D1632173

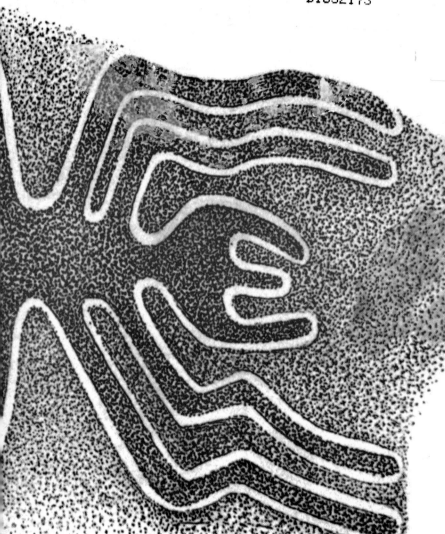

The Book of the
SPIDER

The Book of the SPIDER

From Arachnophobia
to the Love of Spiders

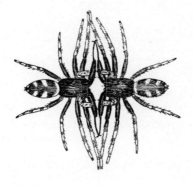

PAUL HILLYARD

HUTCHINSON
LONDON

© Paul Hillyard 1994

The right of Paul Hillyard to be identified as Author of this work has been asserted by Paul Hillyard in accordance with the Copyright, Designs and Patents Act, 1988

1 3 5 7 9 10 8 6 4 2

This edition first published in 1994 by
Hutchinson

Random House UK Ltd
20 Vauxhall Bridge Road, London SW1V 2SA

Random House Australia (Pty) Ltd
20 Alfred Street, Milsons Point, Sydney, NSW 2061, Australia

Random House New Zealand Ltd
18 Poland Road, Glenfield, Auckland 10, New Zealand

Random House South Africa (Pty) Ltd
PO Box 337, Bergvlei, 2012, South Africa

A CIP catalogue record for this book is available from the British Library

ISBN 0 09 177631 7

Set in Bembo Roman by SX Composing Ltd, Rayleigh, Essex
Printed and bound in Great Britain by
Butler and Tanner Ltd, Frome and London

Endpaper illustration: 160 feet (50m) figure
of a spider drawn in the sand at Nazca, Peru

CONTENTS

[v]

The book is dedicated to my wife, Leni.

ACKNOWLEDGEMENTS

The author is grateful to The Natural History Museum in London for permission to publish this book. Access to the Museum's archives and those of University College London (Folklore Library), The British Library, The Museum of Mankind, and St Bartholomew's Hospital London, is gratefully acknowledged.

The author also wishes to thank, for their help and encouragement, colleagues and friends including Caroline Davidson, Anne Baker, Don Macfarlane, Tom Huddleston, John Cloudsley-Thompson, Andrew Smith, John and Frances Murphy, Philip Charpentier, and not forgetting mother and father, Ella and David Hillyard.

And, finally, thanks are due to the excellent team at Hutchinson: Paul Sidey, Dawn Fozard, Tom Gilliatt, Neil Bradford and Alex Hippisley Cox.

PREFACE

When you meet a large spider unexpectedly it is normal to catch your breath. The author of this book is no different from anybody else. What distinguishes me from the squeamish or arachnophobic, however, is my *following* reaction. Instead of trying to flee in horror, I move closer to see it in detail. Nothing pleases me more than to come upon an impressive orb-web with a large spider sitting head-down in the middle. I love to contemplate the aura of menace which seems to surround it. But also, viewing from the best angles according to the light, I study the web and look for whatever is going on in the spider's world.

In search of spiders I have visited islands, mountain tops and remote rainforests. Other places such as neglected churchyards, musty old cellars and grape plantations have also come under scrutiny. If I have the opportunity in tropical countries, I like to inspect the spaces, three to four feet high (one metre), *under* houses. Such habitats can be rewarding, although awkward in terms of backache, and hazardous in terms of dogs, snakes and spiders! It helps to obtain permission first. Back home, in and around London, much of my spider hunting has been done at night in overgrown cemeteries. These can be excellent places to search, as long as one is brave enough to use a torch. At night, the gravestones become the active territories of many spiders which are normally hidden during the day and, against the stonework, they can be seen very easily.

The eerie atmosphere of a cemetery at night is not unlike that of a tropical rainforest – after the noisy chorus of the early night has died down. I have spent several nights camping in the National Park of Malaysia (Taman Negara), which is an ancient rainforest harbouring many attractive but little known species of spiders. Numbers of tourists go to Taman Negara in the hope of catching a glimpse of a tiger but, when I get up in the middle of the night from my tent in the forest, I want to see only spiders.

Walking about under the massive trees, with the aid of a miner's head-lamp, I can spot the tiny eyes of spiders twinkling in the distance. At night it is usual to find that each of the tree trunks has at least one, long-legged 'huntsman spider' (Sparassidae) sitting motionless on the bark. Approach too closely though and it immediately darts round to the other side.

An early ambition of mine was to rediscover the 'ladybird spider' (*Eresus*) in England. Probably many other beginners had similarly dreamed of the glory of finding, once again, this elusive beauty. According to the books, it had been last seen in 1906 on heaths in Dorset which had long since been built over. However, there was also a mysterious association with Kynance Cove in Cornwall, because of an apparent sighting there in 1932. And surely, that sighting must have been genuine because such an unusual spider could hardly be mistaken; with its red body and black spots the male mimics a ladybird, while the female, without any resemblance to a ladybird, is much bigger and entirely black. Typically this species inhabits hot stony places in southern Europe. But unfortunately alas, the British rediscovery was not to be mine. While I was searching the south-facing Cornish coves, the news came that a small population of ladybird spiders had been found on a heath in Dorset. The find, in 1979, had been made by beetle hunters who were, of course, puzzled by this strange-looking spider, and quite unaware of the glory!

I had more luck when observing spiders in Spain. I came across the web of a female 'wasp spider' (*Argiope*) in which she was closely attended by two males. The trio had arranged themselves very photogenically and so I duly took a couple of photographs. But then the female dropped from her position and adopted an unnatural, sickly-looking pose. I wondered if I had done something wrong. Had I disturbed it? Then, about five minutes later, an event occurred which was imperceptible to me but which triggered immediate excitement among the males. They started chasing each other rapidly around the web. The

reason for this soon became apparent: the female was beginning
to moult to her final, sexually mature stage – the very moment
the males had been waiting for. I continued to take photos.
Possibly that critical event had been the first crack in the female's
old skin (exoskeleton), or maybe her release of a chemical signal
or pheromone. After about twenty minutes the old skin had
been shed but before the female had fully regained her
composure, one of the males succeeded in mating with her.
Unfortunately though, he failed to withdraw quickly enough,
and became trussed up in silk . . . to be eaten later by the female.

It might be supposed that only eccentrics are interested in
spiders. This is not true, though admittedly some characters do
indulge in making large collections of live tarantulas, most of
which are bought from dealers. Some collectors go so far as to
keep tarantulas in every room in their home, and undoubtedly
this can be grounds for divorce. However, the world of spiders
is so diverse that there is wide scope for all levels of interest. The
adventurous can search for unusual spiders in exotic places. On a
more domestic level, one might happily settle down to learn
about the spiders which live in a local park or nature reserve.
Britain is very well served in that it is relatively easy to obtain
books which describe all the country's species. Currently, spider
spotters are being invited to participate in the National House
Spiders Survey of Great Britain which is organised by the South
West University at Plymouth, Devon. This survey will try to
answer such questions as: Do spiders prefer old or new, terraced
or detached houses, cottages or blocks of flats? Do they prefer
heated or unheated rooms? Do the greatest numbers live in
cellars, lofts, garages or sheds? Contributors are thus presently
looking into baths, under beds, and behind boilers, etc. to log
information on the habits and domiciles of British house spiders.
The eventual result should tell us something about the spiders,
and also something about ourselves!

My work, at the Natural History Museum in London,
involves maintaining the national collection of spiders but also

includes advising on the human aspects or, rather, on the problems which occur when humans and spiders meet. After a week in 1988 of unusual numbers of spiders imported in grapes, I was visited at the Museum by the worried presidents of two grape-growing companies, one from California and the other from Spain. A couple of days later, on my first tour of a Spanish grape plantation, it was immediately easy to understand why the spiders chose their particular habitats. *Outside* the plantation, in the surrounding countryside, there was great heat and dryness but *inside*, under the canopy of vine leaves, the conditions were very pleasant. In the dappled sunlight, the humid air was warm and still and although most of the grapes had been harvested, those that remained were overripe and busy with clouds of fruit flies. It was a magnet for spiders and, of course, by feeding on the pests they were doing much more good than harm. Unfortunately, the typical supermarket customer who discovers spiders in their fruit usually does not see it from this point of view. So a person who likes spiders, as I do, is called upon to advise on how they may be eradicated.

The Book of the
SPIDER

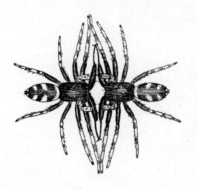

CHAPTER ONE

ARACHNOPHOBIA

Little Miss Muffet
Sat on a tuffet,
Eating of curds and whey
There came a big spider,
And sat down beside her,
And frightened Miss Muffet away

MOTHER GOOSE

Miss Patience Muffet, probably the real 'Little Miss Muffet', suffered greatly because her father, the Reverend Dr Thomas Muffet, or Mouffet (1553–1604), had an excessive fondness for spiders. He loved to encourage the house spider because, in his opinion, 'she doth beautifie with her tapestry and hangings'. Furthermore, he was keen on treating his daughter with spiders to cure many ailments. No doubt the poor girl was horribly traumatised by spiders and thus it would be no surprise at all (though history does not record) if in fact Miss Muffet went on to develop a full-blown case of arachnophobia.[1]

Arachnophobia, or the fear of spiders, is the classic example of an animal phobia. It can afflict anybody, even the toughest

[1] W. S. Bristowe, however, expressed doubt about the verse. Apparently Dr Mouffet's diary described a picnic in Epping Forest near London when he was forced to flee from some enraged wasps. The implication is that he was the 'Miss Muffet' and the wasps were changed to a spider to help the rhyme.

and most macho of men. Many people have it to a mild degree but in serious cases it can totally disrupt the life of the sufferer, who is never able to relax, even at home. All the rooms in the house will need to be checked repeatedly just in case a spider has appeared. And before going to sleep, the bedroom will have to be searched thoroughly, preferably armed with a can of pesticide. Better still, someone else will be good enough to search the room and declare it safe. One sufferer has confessed: 'I couldn't even write the word *spider*. I daren't put my handbag on the floor in case a spider crawled into it . . . I could never go into a room until someone else had made sure there were no spiders inside.'

In countries with only fairly innocuous kinds of spiders, arachnophobia seems to be a completely irrational fear. Compared with the dangers of road traffic, most spiders are totally insignificant. But that is a rational argument and many phobic individuals do in fact recognise that there is no need to fear them. Often their phobia is not a fear of what spiders may do, but simply a loathing of the sight of the creature. Unfortunately, the irrational nature of arachnophobia causes the sufferers extra grief because 'normal' people cannot understand the depth of their fears.

A woman who claimed not to be arachnophobic once wrote to the author: 'There is something about spiders, they seem to be aware of us, unlike insects who seem to be oblivious of our existence. I always wake to the feeling that there is someone or something in the room, and sure enough it is usually a large spider on the wall or ceiling just above me, sort of watching.'

DIFFERENT KINDS OF ARACHNOPHOBIA

In countries such as Australia, and also in parts of the USA, the fear of spiders may be extreme but it is usually focused on particular venomous species. In countries like Britain where it is well known that the native species are virtually harmless, but which happen to include some rather large and intrusive house-spiders, the fear is of more abstract qualities such as 'spideriness'. The arachnophobic British were on full alert in 1988, when newspaper headlines about foreign spiders imported in grapes caused nationwide panic among shoppers and resulted in the destruction of huge quantities of perfectly edible fruit.

While such an exaggerated response may seem to be a quirk of modern, urban life, with its lack of natural hazards, the fear of spiders does nevertheless have a long history. Two thousand years ago 'a dreadful plague of spiders' caused the depopulation of lands in Abyssinia and, during the Middle Ages, spiders were blamed for long episodes of mass hysteria (see The Story of Tarantism, page 55). Considering the world's primitive cultures, arachnophobia is manifested in various forms in some but appears to be completely absent in others. For example, in Africa, tribal people are generally afraid of large, troublesome spiders but their greater fear is for the witch doctor's judgement. He will probably declare that a spider's bite is the sign of a curse on the victim. And in the case of some of the Amazonian people, there is no discernible fear at all. The Piaroa Indians actually collect the largest tarantula spiders and eat them, by the dozen.

CASE HISTORIES

Cases of arachnophobia typically affect the middle-aged or elderly. The ratio of cases is approximately nine female to every one male, though it is probable that men are less willing to admit their problem. A large hospital in London, such as St Bartholomew's, is likely to treat about five cases per year. While the phobia is more frequent among adults than children, there seems to be a common agreement that it does often originate in childhood, when a general fear of spiders and insects, as opposed to other more 'cuddly' animals, is considered to be normal. Most children grow out of their fear but when it does persist into adulthood it tends to worsen and rarely disappears without treatment. Apparently, the most difficult phobias to treat and eliminate are those acquired when adult.

Adult arachnophobia is often traceable back to earlier traumatic experiences with spiders. At school, a sensitive child might have been singled out for jokes with spiders and presented with specimens, in matchboxes or bottles of milk, just so that all around could laugh at their horrified reaction. Other sufferers might, for example, recall memories of an uncle or aunt who threw the tops of tomatoes at them, while calling, 'Watch out, spider!' Worse still, the evil uncle might have threatened the child with imprisonment in the garden shed . . . *where there are so many large spiders!* In fact, many adults have used the fear of spiders to discourage children from going to forbidden places.

The case of a young man in his twenties began when, as a child, he had nothing more than the usual aversion to 'creepy crawlies'. Unfortunately at school he was victimised and tormented with spiders put down the back of his neck. He developed a severe arachnophobia and became totally dependent on his mother to act as a 'rescuer'. If he met a spider, instead of fleeing as others would, his reaction was to freeze until the rescuer came to deal with it. On one occasion he remained 'frozen' for ten hours. He had a mania for checking the rooms in the house and this became highly ritualised. Before entering a room he would look carefully round the door and examine each wall in a precise order. The ultimate horror that he feared was to go into the bathroom and discover a spider sitting on the door which had just closed behind him. Things became worse when his mother also developed arachnophobia and could no longer act as his rescuer. At that point, being unable to contemplate life on his own, he was forced to seek treatment.

ASSESSING ATTITUDES TOWARDS SPIDERS

When 18,000 children answered a BBC question in the 1950s: 'Which animal do you dislike most?' – the snake came first with 27 per cent of the replies, the spider second with 10 per cent, and the lion third with 4.5 per cent. When the survey was repeated in 1988 the spider was again the second most unpopular animal, but this time after the rat. In an American survey (Fish and Wildlife Service) conducted at schools during the early 1980s, the spider was hardly mentioned; its place in the unpopularity stakes was taken by the cockroach.

Theodore Savory, a teacher at a female college in England, who had a lifelong interest in spiders, asked his students over a period of twelve years this question: 'Are you afraid of spiders and why?' The great majority said 'yes', and their fears fell into three groups: (1) the fear of large spiders; (2) the fear of black spiders; and (3) the fear of long-legged spiders. Savory also cited the rapid unpredictable movements of spiders but *not* their bite. Doubtless it would be different in countries like Brazil and Australia where the replies to such a survey would surely include the fear of the spider's bite. The attitudes towards spiders in a particular country reflect the local culture as well as the perceived threat. A curious phenomenon among people generally, however, is that the mind tends to magnify, and double, the size of spiders.

Primo Levi, the survivor from Auschwitz who was himself somewhat arachnophobic, tried hard to answer the basic question: Why do people fear spiders? Levi believed that it is usual to blame the spider's eight legs but he wanted to know: who stops to count them? He thus considered many other possible reasons, for example: that spiders are cruel; that they are ugly and hairy; that they lie in ambush; and that they suddenly appear on the scene in a furtive way. Levi dismissed all such 'reasons' as the cause of arachnophobia and he added that some others are no more than academic. For example, how many humans have actually seen a female spider devour a male after mating – and been affected by it?

ANALYSES AND THEORIES

For centuries it was believed that a mother frightened by a spider during pregnancy would pass on the fear to the child. While this is no longer believed to be so, children can acquire the phobia from their parents and from stories about spiders with unnatural abilities, particularly those that could torment humans. People suffer needlessly because they have been told, for example, that spiders can appear unexpectedly from the bath's drainpipe, that they are immune to drowning, and that they are just waiting to attack the next bather and, horror of horrors, run across their bare skin. The key defence of arachnophobes is *avoidance*, avoiding the bathroom in particular. But each time that avoidance is taken, it tends to reinforce the phobia. And associated objects may also become feared: a person may fear a room with cobwebs, then a cupboard with cobwebs, and finally, the cupboard itself. One woman undergoing treatment was introduced to a large tarantula spider but this only increased her fear and gave her a secondary phobia towards the building in which she was being treated.

Among the population as a whole, there exists a wide range of attitudes to spiders from enjoyment to mild aversion and, in extreme cases, to terror. In Britain about half of all women and 10 per cent of men express at least some fear of spiders. Figure 1 shows the range of attitudes among adults towards spiders and insects. It has been estimated that the groups at the opposite ends of the spectrum, i.e. (i) those that enjoy spiders and insects and (ii) those that definitely do not, are both relatively rare – each involves about 3 per cent of the population. The remaining 94 per cent ranges from those who are indifferent to those who are fearful, although not to a degree compatible with true phobia.

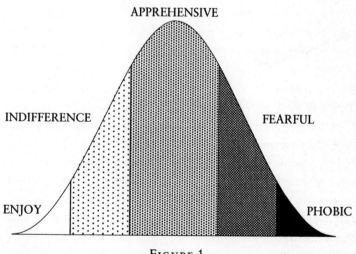

FIGURE 1

What is a phobia? It is an anxiety or fear which is out of proportion to the danger of the situation. Its symptoms are similar to those of the normal fear response: sudden apprehension, loss of control, shortness of breath, increased heart rate, faintness, trembling and sweaty palms. In extreme cases the individual can become paralysed. A phobic reaction may be separated into three components: (i) subjective (feelings of fear), (ii) autonomic (physiological responses) and (iii) motor (immobilisation or flight). Some typical reactions are seen in the following examples: A woman screamed when she discovered a spider at home and ran out to find a neighbour to remove it. She was trembling with fear and had to keep the neighbour at her side for two hours before she could remain at home alone again. Another woman found herself on top of the fridge but without any recollection of getting there. As Sigmund Freud (1865–1939) said, 'What in general appears to us strange in these phobias is not so much their content as their intensity.'

After it was realised that all sufferers from phobias can be genuinely described as ill, doctors, psychiatrists and others have sought to understand these conditions and devise a cure. One early school of thought believed that phobias represented unconscious mental conflicts. Accordingly, traditional Freudian psychoanalysts have attempted to explain phobias by means of relating them to underlying factors such as a desire for the mother's attention or a fear of the father. In arachnophobia, according to Freud, the fear of the bite of a spider represented the fear of punishment. In such cases, the dread of the father had become transferred to the spider.

Today, while such psychoanalytical theories are not commonly accepted, some practitioners still talk in terms of 'underlying causes' and 'symptoms of inner disturbance'. Patients are told to 'remove the emotion and the phobia will go', or to 're-live the original cause to get over the symptom'. Interpreted in this way, the phobia is a symptom of some other problem and is not actually caused by spiders! It has even been claimed that arachnophobia is really a sexual problem – in that hair on the body has a sexual significance and thus the repression of sex may be expressed in the fear of hairy spiders.

Phobias are often very difficult to explain. Queen Elizabeth I had the 'heart and stomach of a King' but, apparently, she was afraid of roses. One recent advance in understanding is the discovery that arachnophobic people are sensitive to the mere suggestion of 'spideriness'. In a study which used cards printed with spidery words in different coloured inks, two groups of people, 'arachnophobes' and 'normal', were asked to look at the cards and name the colours. The words were *hairy, legs, creepy, crawl* and *spider*. The study's findings revealed that arachnophobes took far longer to name the colours than did normal people; they felt anxious and could not think clearly about the colours of the words.

There are, perhaps, two basic, underlying reasons why people develop arachnophobia. First, there may be an inherited tendency within a family to be anxious or nervous and to have fears such as those of spiders. Second, there may have been a *conditioning* through which the person has learnt to be afraid of spiders or has had unpleasant experiences with them. In a survey at American high schools it was found that the study of biology tended to awaken animal phobias. Of the biology students, 53 per cent had a fear of animals, while only 35 per cent of the students taking other courses shared this kind of fear. Nevertheless, most cures for arachnophobia are based on the principle that what is learnt can be unlearnt. The experience of the Insect House at London Zoo is that education and familiarisation with spiders can indeed overcome the phobia.

A third explanation, claimed by some, is that arachnophobes are more than usually repelled by dirt and disgusting creatures such as slugs, cockroaches and maggots. Undoubtedly, it is true that the general dislike of insects, or entomophobia, is often related to a desire for cleanliness. According to this 'unclean' theory, arachnophobia originated in medieval Europe where the presence of spiders was associated with houses infected with bubonic plague. The homes of the dead and dying fell into neglect and the spiders moved in, acting as tell-tale signs of infection. It is further claimed that the memory of this has passed on from generation to generation.

Thus sufferers are likely to have a phobic relative. Indeed, a tendency to inherit the fear is generally accepted by most experts. Recent research has found that this tendency arises from an altered function in a part of the brain – a specific pathway, which holds out the possibility that it might be capable of being targeted with a particular drug.

THERAPEUTIC TREATMENT

'Aversion' or 'behaviour' therapy is today the standard treatment for arachnophobia. The particular form of the therapy will depend on the therapist, the age of the patient, and the extent of the problem. Usually it will involve some sort of 'exposure' to spiders combined with ample moral support. Successful treatments are likely to involve giving reassurance, encouragement without undue pressure, and feedback on the level of fear to give the individual more rational control. A dramatically different approach is known as 'implosive theory'. With the help of images, the patient is asked to visualise a confrontation with the feared object along the lines of . . . 'imagine you are a fly trapped in the sticky web of an enormous spider'. According to this theory, the anxiety should habituate or disappear following such sessions. In reality, it is much more likely that the phobia will worsen. In modern therapeutic practice, most patients will instead begin a course of gradual 'desensitisation'. And these days, few patients will be given, as in the past, a drug therapy involving muscle relaxants or tranquillizers.

Desensitisation is a progressive exposure to a series of spiders which are increasingly difficult for the patient. The material may take the form of pictures or of specimens in a range of sizes from tiny to very large. The programme might begin with no more than just bits of dead spiders; later, live spiders may be used. After exposure to a small, inoffensive spider that is

not scary, the patient should become habituated to it and be able to move up to the next level. Many will be given specimens to carry around with them in their bag. The objective is that with increasing familiarity spiders will no longer be able to shock the person.

Finally, the sufferer needs to be shown that their dearly held but distorted ideas about spiders are simply wrong. Suitable education may be got at a zoo or natural history museum. It needs to be borne in mind, however, that progress can easily be reversed if confidence is still only fragile. One brave woman, who was determined to conquer her fear, visited a large museum collection with her therapist. The woman was guided around the spider collection on a route carefully chosen to include only the smaller, inoffensive kinds. During the tour, it became obvious that she had suffered for years partly because of her many misapprehensions and sheer ignorance of spiders. Learning a little about them, she began to make real progress. Until, that was, the therapist gleefully exclaimed: 'Oh, look at that monster over there!' At this point the patient lost her nerve and hurried out.

Though it may be difficult to contemplate, the best form of self-help is to learn about spiders and to know that they are essentially innocent. Arachnophobia is a fear of the unknown. It helps greatly to be able to predict their habits based on a true understanding of their behaviour and capabilities. It also helps to know about practical measures: for example, that spiders can be prevented from getting inside by blocking entry points such as windows, grilles, and the gaps under doors. And finally, one should give up any thoughts of fumigation because this expensive treatment is not the solution.

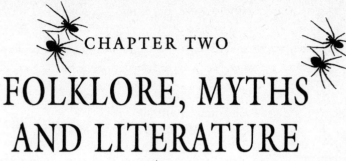

CHAPTER TWO

FOLKLORE, MYTHS AND LITERATURE

THE UNNATURAL HISTORY
OF THE SPIDER

Many animals have associations with simple human attributes – foxes are cunning, owls are wise, and elephants never forget. Spiders on the other hand seem to be the 'Jekylls and Hydes' of the animal world. They are both admired and loathed, sometimes at the same time. We praise their industry but we also harbour a deep-rooted fear of their venom and their alien lives. The parts spiders play in stories, poems, and superstitions are greatly contrasting. Sometimes the spider is depicted as sensitive, skilful and wise, but at other times as the villain. It is similar with their webs: these are portrayed as objects of inspired and beautiful engineering, but also as symbols of desertion and untrustworthiness.

> O what a tangled web we weave,
> When at first we practise to deceive!
> Sir Walter Scott

Of all the 'minibeasts' in children's stories, creatures such as ants, beetles, snails and caterpillars, the spider seems to be one of the most, if not the most popular. Many cultures around the world have a place for spiders in their folklore and it is remarkable how many seem to have had the same idea – that it is unlucky or unwise to kill a spider unnecessarily. Perhaps it is true to say that spiders capture our imagination because they are small and yet so clever in laying their traps.

> When I'm hanging head-down in my web.
> That's when I do my thinking
>   E. B. WHITE, *Charlotte's Web*

Spider lore may be classified according to a number of themes: spiders are believed to be bringers of luck; they are able to forecast the weather and predict events; and they are revered in a variety of religious beliefs. In the past they have had medicinal uses. It must also be admitted that they are associated with evil. The qualities of spiders are indeed complex – but the way they are viewed depends on the circumstances and people's attitudes; there are no 'absolute truths' in this chapter.

THE STORY OF ARACHNE

The spider mythology of Europe began with the story of Arachne, as told by the Roman poet, Ovid, in his *Metamorphoses*. Arachne was a country girl renowned throughout the region of Lydia in Ancient Greece, for her skill in spinning and weaving. Her teacher was Athene, the goddess of wisdom, also known as Pallas. However, as Arachne span and weaved the finest tapestries and fabrics, a great rivalry grew between them. Athene became jealous of her pupil. So Athene disguised herself as a withered old woman and visited the girl at her loom. Expressing admiration, the old woman asked who was her teacher. When the boastful Arachne denied that it had been Athene, the goddess dropped her disguise and revealed her true identity. Flushed with anger, she said, 'Those who defy the gods must make good their words. We will have a spinning contest to see who weaves the finer tapestry!'

News of the contest spread quickly and from all over Lydia people came to watch. Athene proceeded to make a tapestry with the design of an Olympic scene in which Nemesis, the goddess of vengeance, carried away those who dared challenge the Immortals. The tapestry was very fine. But Arachne's tapestry was even more beautiful and elaborate. She depicted scenes of the misbehaviour of the gods and goddesses, of seduction, and of the unworthy tricks they played when they wanted their way. The work was perfect. Even Athene could not find a flaw in it.

Angered by Arachne's skill and impertinence, Athene became enraged. Her hands tore at the tapestry, and she beat Arachne about the head with a shuttle. In her distress, Arachne turned away from the horrified gaze of the onlookers. She ran to the woods, put a rope around her neck and tried to end her life. Then Athene took pity on her mortal rival and, being a powerful goddess, she granted her a new life as a spider, the weaver with the ultimate skill in spinning. 'Live on wicked one,' Athene said, 'but always hanging, and let posterity share your punishment.' Arachne's body changed into that of a spider and she was thus doomed to spin and weave for ever.

> Pallas was angry, and in wroth she said,
> Yet live and hang thou proud and haughty Mayd,
> And that thou mayst still suffer 'tis my minde,
> The same Law lasts for thee and all thy kinde.
>
> IN REV. E. TOPSELL, 1607

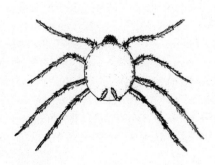

The word *Arachne* (Greek for 'spider') is the basis of the name *Arachnida* – 'spider-like' – the Class to which spiders belong. 'Arachnologists' are specialists in the Class. The Latin name for spider is *aranea*; the French *araignée*; the Italian *arágna*; and the Spanish *araña*; all show a more or less direct derivation from the Greek word. The English word, *spider*, comes probably from the Anglo-Saxon *spinnan*, to spin. The German name is *Spinne* (*spinnen* being to spin), and the Swedish is *Spindel*.

SPIDERS BRING GOOD LUCK

The association of spiders with the spinning of new clothes is the basis of a widespread superstition. A spider found running over one's clothes is believed to have come to spin new ones. It is not a big jump in imagination to go from new clothes, to a present, and from a present, to the arrival of a stranger bearing gifts or, in the modern world, money – thus *money spider*. Many superstitions like this have owed their survival to the fact that their observance is only a small price to pay to avoid disaster, or to benefit from the chance of good luck. Frank Gibson wrote in his book *Superstitions about Animals* (1904): 'Even timid ladies, who would faint were any creeping thing to touch them, will allow the money spider to crawl upon them with impunity, hoping that by permitting it to do so, some form of good luck will ensue.'

A great many cultures around the world seem to have had the same idea – that spiders bring good luck and, conversely, that to kill one brings bad luck. On meeting a spider one is generally recommended to throw it carefully over the shoulder or merely to let it go in peace. In England, if a money spider is caught and thrown over the shoulder, the person will come into wealth – unless he or she looks to see where the spider landed! In Kentucky, if a spider comes close, it should be picked up and put in one's pocket since it will bring money. And to be on the safe side, a dead spider should always be carried in one's shoe.

In 1936, a policeman on duty at Lambeth Bridge in London held up heavy traffic in order to let a large spider cross the road. He was cheered by the passers-by. Even today, people who neither like spiders nor believe themselves to be superstitious, find it strangely difficult to tread on one. In the home, many will avoid killing a spider, preferring instead to remove it carefully, using a glass and card at arm's length – while reciting the Old English nursery rhyme:

> If you wish to live and thrive,
> Let the spider run alive.

and not forgetting:

> Kill a spider and bad luck yours will be,
> Until of flies you've swatted fifty three.

Some superstitions depend on the exact movements of the spiders. In England a spider descending on a thread towards you is an omen of an approaching visitor or present. In China a spider at the end of a long thread denotes the arrival of a friend from a far distance. In Japan a spider hanging from a thread, with legs drawn in, signifies a visitor with a present, but if its legs are outstretched the visitor will arrive empty handed. In Puerto Rico it is unlucky to see a spider dropping down on a thread but lucky to see one climbing up. And if you find one crawling on your bed, it means that a stranger is coming; if you kill the spider, they will not come. In many of these superstitions the colour of the specimen is also significant – black spiders are usually bad, and pale ones good.

In Kentucky, to go through a spider's web and break it across the face means that a happy day is approaching – it brings good luck to a bride, and the bride who finds a spider on her wedding dress may consider herself blessed. However, a spider on the neck denotes a secret lover! For the sake of future happiness and prosperity, Hindus in Bengal collect spiders and scatter them like confetti at weddings. The Bhils and Mats of India, during marriages, actually worship an effigy of the spider. And in Egypt, good fortune is not left to chance. A spider is carefully placed in the bed of a married couple on their wedding night.

But not everyone believes that spiders bring good luck. It used to be said in New England . . . *'With every spider you kill, you kill an enemy!'*

RELIGIOUS MYTHOLOGY

The myths of many ancient peoples tell of the spider as the creator of the world. Depending on the particular belief, the spider inhabited the underworld, or lived in the sky. A widespread image is that of the monstrous mother spider, with a huge abdomen out of proportion to her legs, producing eggs *ad infinitum.*

In the mythology of many native Americans, the spider was the original force in nature because of its mastery of weaving. According to the legends of the Pueblo and Navajo people: 'In the beginning there was nothing but *Spider Woman* . . . no other living creature, no bird or animal or fish yet lived, in the dark purple light that glowed at the Dawn of Being . . .' Spider Woman created people from the clay of the earth, and to each she attached a thread of web connected to her. It is said that Spider Woman still lives in the holes of 'Spider Rock' among the rocks in Navajo land. Navajo Indian mothers warn unmanageable children that the great Spider Woman will clamber down her silken ladder to truss them up and carry them back to her lair. The whitened bones of previous victims glinting at the top of the rock show this to be true.

A Navajo legend also tells of a young girl who saw a wisp of smoke coming from a hole in the ground. At the bottom of the hole sat Spider Woman spinning a web. The girl was invited inside to learn how to weave blankets and baskets. But she was warned that bad luck would follow if a hole, representing Spider Woman's burrow, was not placed in the middle of each article. Thus to this day, the blankets and baskets of the Navajos have the hole, though sometimes it is cleverly disguised.

Many tribes in Borneo worship the spider as a primordial god. According to one legend, the mother spider wove a web over the earth and worked with a larva to nourish the roots of the original tree, from the branches of which, came their human ancestors. In West African mythology, the spider's thread represents a sort of umbilical cord between God in the sky and humans on earth. For other peoples it is a medium for ascending into the celestial heights. In Polynesia an elaborate myth has come about where spiders' silk forms a ladder or tree which ascends into the heavens. In one version of this legend, a young man, Tawhaki, decided to return to the sky-world after living, and suffering, on earth. He ascended a mountain and climbed a tree growing on its summit. From the tree, a great spider's web extended up to the sky. Tawhaki climbed up the web. Twice it broke, causing him to fall, but on the third attempt he succeeded in reaching the sky.

The belief that the spirit of man passes at death into the body of an animal is widespread in the world. Cunninghame Graham, in his book *Conquest of New Granada*, related that spiders were sacred to the Chibchas who believe that human souls, after death, make their way, through dark and tortuous passages, to the centre of the earth. Before arriving at the centre, however, they have to cross a river on rafts of spiders' webs. Without these rafts, they cannot cross the river and so will remain in perpetual limbo. Thus, to kill a spider is to kill a soul. In West Africa, a baboon spider, which lives in burrows, is believed to be in touch with the underworld where dwell the spirits of the ancestors. If a child crushes a spider by accident he cries, 'Bad luck! I have killed my mother.' Similarly, the Teton Indians of

North America try not to kill spiders lest their spirits should avenge them. But, if a Teton Indian does chance to kill a spider he is careful to say: 'O, Grandfather Spider the Thunder-Beings killed you.' This is so that its spirit will not tell the other spiders who was to blame!

BELIEFS AROUND THE WORLD

Spiders were mentioned in early Chinese writings. They were associated with the toad, centipede, snake and scorpion to form the group of the Wu Tu, the five poisonous animals. However, in China, spiders have also been looked upon favourably. They are regarded as apostles of Confucius and thus possessed of much wisdom – because wooden tablets dedicated to Confucius are often selected as a site for their webs. In fact Chinese legends involving spiders often emphasise the webs. According to a story from the Tsin Dynasty (c. 2,000 years ago), a handsome monk named Tang Seng made a long pilgrimage to India. On the way he encountered the Seven Spider Fairy Sisters who made huge webs in order to bind their enemies and trap good-looking men. In fact they caught Tang Seng and wanted to marry him. When he refused, they tried instead to eat him. It was indeed lucky that he and his companion were able to fight them off.

The Etruscans (Italy) were great believers in the use of symbols and amulets to ward off evil. For them the spider was sacred to Mercury and its image was engraved on precious stones worn as a talisman for shrewdness in business matters. The Ancient Egyptians, however, appear to have ignored spiders almost completely. Instead, they venerated the scorpion and were greatly absorbed in the activities of insects, especially scarab beetles. In Europe long ago the Garden or Diadem Spider (*Araneus diadematus*) was revered because of the white cross on its back. In Japan, the Great Spider God used to be hailed as a brilliant military strategist.

By a remarkable coincidence, or else by a common ancestry that goes back over many millennia, the same practice of using spiders in divination occurs from Africa to Indonesia. In Cameroon, and also in Bali, small twigs are arranged around the entrance to the burrow of a large tarantula or baboon spider. A small dish of rice wine is offered to the spider and positioned near by. The whole site is protected by bamboo sticks. In Cameroon the practice has been described by Eric de Rosny: in the early morning, the witch doctor inspects the twigs to see if the spider's nocturnal movements have brought them to new positions relative to the burrow. According to the new arrangement, the witch doctor is then able to divine future events and discover hidden knowledge.

SPIDERS IN THE BIBLE AND THE KORAN

In the Bible there are three references to the spider. Two of them use the spider's web as an emblem of fragility, of little value and easily destroyed. In the Book of Job (8:13–14) it is said that the 'trust' of the ungodly shall be the equivalent of a spider's web: '. . . the hypocrite's hope shall perish: . . . whose trust shall be a spider's web'. Isaiah (59:5) speaks of the futile plotting of evildoers, 'they . . . weave the spider's web'. The following proverb is from the Old Testament Book of Proverbs (30:28) (In the Good News Bible the spider has become the gecko):

> There be four things which are little upon the earth
> > But they are exceeding wise;
> > The ants are a people not strong,

Yet they prepare their meat in the summer;
The conies are but a feeble folk,
Yet they make their houses in the rocks;
The locusts have no king,
Yet they go forth all of them by bands;
The spider taketh hold with her hands,
And is in kings' palaces.

Spiders are very common in the Bible lands, though as usual, the webs are more easily seen than the spiders themselves. Undoubtedly, the local version of the black widow spider (*Latrodectus tredecimguttatus*) has always been numerous there. Bartholomew in the Authorised or King James Version (1611) assured readers that: 'The venomous spider is a little creeping beast with many feet ... Against all biting of spiders, the remedy is flies stamped and laid to the biting, draweth out the venom and abateth the ache and sore.'

In the Koran, in Sura XXIX 'The Spider', it is written: 'The likeness of those who choose guardians other than Allah, or God, is as the likeness of the spider who buildeth a house: but the very frailest of all houses surely is the house of the spider. Did they but know this' (Rodwel translation, 1909). Thus it is warned that those who depart from the faith are on an unstable foundation, insecure as a spider's web. However, no antipathy towards spiders is intended; in the Moslem tradition the spider is revered and should never be destroyed.

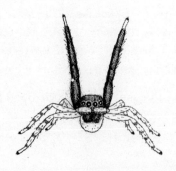

FUGITIVES SAVED BY SPIDERS

King Robert the Bruce of Scotland, after his defeat by King Edward of England in 1306, was lying exhausted in a barn but, upon looking up, he spied a 'wee beastie' trying to swing from one beam of the roof to the next, in a valiant attempt to anchor the first line of its web. Six times the spider tried and six times it failed. 'Now shall this spider (said Bruce) teach me what I am to do, for I also have failed six times.' The spider made a seventh effort and finally succeeded. Its perseverance inspired Bruce – 'if at first you don't succeed, try, try again'. From that moment the course of history changed – Bruce emerged from hiding, rallied his men, and in one last attempt defeated Edward's army at Bannockburn in 1314. The story of Bruce and the spider has become a classic in the English-speaking world.

In many countries, folklore tells of a hero who escaped his pursuers because a spider had built a web across the entrance to his hiding place, and so they thought he could not be inside. In ancient Hebrew writing (interpreted by France and Hosking), the spider was an example of an apparently futile creature which did nevertheless have a purpose:

> David doubted God's wisdom in having created such a useless creature that busies itself spinning a web that has no value. But when David was being pursued by Saul and took refuge in a cave, God sent a spider to weave its web across

the opening and Saul called his men away saying that it was useless to search within, since the web showed that no one could have entered. Thus David's life was saved by the tiny creature he had scorned.

In a similar way, it is said that Mohammed, when he fled Mecca, owed his escape from the Coreishites to a spider which had spun its web across the mouth of the cave in which he was hiding. In Japan, the twelfth-century hero, Yoritomo, was saved from his enemies by a spider's web spun across the opening of a hollow tree in which he sheltered.

> With spiders I had friendship made,
> And watch'd them in their sullen trade
>
> BYRON, *The Prisoner of Chillon*

SPIDERS AS SYMBOLS OF EVIL

> 'Will you walk into my parlour?' said the spider to the fly;
> 'Tis the prettiest little parlour that ever you did spy.
> The way into my parlour is up a winding stair,
> And I have many curious things to show when you are
> there.'
> 'Oh no, no,' said the little fly, 'to ask me is in vain,
> For who goes up your winding stair can ne'er come down
> again.'
>
> MARY HOWITT, *The Spider and the Fly* (1821)

It is disconcerting the way spiders leisurely build their traps and expect their victims to come to them. It is also an unpleasant fact that spiders deal with their prey by using an 'evil' method, poison. Just the sight of an enormous black spider, a ubiquitous symbol of horror, is enough to cause immediate, wide-eyed fear. Carl Jung said that the appearance of spiders in dreams is a

[26]

sign of an unconscious obsession with suicide. Many have also believed that the presence of spiders goes hand in hand with sickness, or plague; they were even reputed to cause cancer.

In Freudian terms, the spider is said to symbolise the mother. For men, because of their castration complex, spiders may also signify the fear of dangerous females. Such fears arise out of a feeling of inferiority to the mother and to women generally.

> The capturing technique of the spider who covers with filaments the prey caught in the web supposedly turns it into a maternal symbol: the spider is the enemy-mother who envelops and encompasses, who wants to make us re-enter the womb from which we have issued, bind us tightly to take us back to the impotence of infancy, subject us again to her power; and there are those who remember that in almost all languages the spider's name is feminine, that the larger and more beautiful webs are those of the female spiders.
>
> PRIMO LEVI (1989)

Consciously or otherwise, we often associate spider with female. We have for example the story of Arachne and Athene, on the one hand the industrious girl, and on the other, the all-powerful goddess. In the spider kingdom chauvinism is the other way round. Those female spiders which have the habit of devouring their mates after love making are likely to be applauded by ardent feminists. Shakespeare used spiders to compare them with the supposed sexual cunning of women:

> Here in her hairs
> The painter plays the spider, and hath woven
> A golden mesh t'entrap the hearts of men
> SHAKESPEARE, *The Merchant of Venice*, Act III, Scene II

W. H. Hudson, in his book *The Naturalist in La Plata*, recorded the local inhabitants' great fear of spiders – in a cowboy's ballad which told of how Cordoba (Argentina) was once invaded by an army of monstrous spiders. The townspeople went out with drums beating and flags flying to repel the invasion but, after firing several volleys, they were forced to turn and run for their lives . . . Such a tendency of exaggerating the deadly nature of spiders has a long history. In Anglo-Saxon, the word for spider was *Attercop*, meaning 'poison-head'. It was generally believed that spiders could gather poison from flowers as bees gather honey. The old English proverb, 'Where the bee gathereth honey, the spider sucks poison' was recalled by Sir Thomas Wyatt (1503–42) in the following verse:

> Nature, that gave the bee so feate a grace
> To find honey of so wondrous fashion,
> Hath taught the spider out of the same place
> To fetch poyson by strange alteracion.

At the trial of the Countess of Essex for the murder of Sir Thomas Overbury, in the time of Shakespeare, it was learnt that the Countess had procured from one of the witnesses seven large spiders, as the strongest and most deadly poison that could be obtained. In Turkestan it is reputed that local wine brewed from the bodies of spiders soaked in alcohol can bring on paralysis in half an hour. Victims, usually thirsty travellers, were said by Gustav Krist, in *Alone through the Forbidden Land*, to be then thrown to the bears.

FORECASTING THE WEATHER

Among English country folk, it is generally believed that an abundance of webs on the grass in the morning foretells good weather. A very welcome sight is that of many orb-webs with spiders at their hub or centre, or sheet-webs with their owners sitting at the mouths of their tubular retreats. If an orb-web weaver starts building after the rain has ceased, one may be confident that no further rain is expected. Building the web in the evening means that a fine night and morning will follow. Short stay lines attached to orb-webs are said to be a bad sign, and long stay lines a good one. In many countries, the entry of large numbers of spiders into houses is believed to herald the approach of severe weather. In Scandinavia it used to be said that the height above ground at which spiders make their nests, on stalks of standing corn, would indicate the depth of snow in the winter to come.

In North America, Europe and elsewhere, spider activity is associated with good weather. On fine, sunny mornings, especially during the autumn, lines of spider silk, or gossamer, are wafted upwards on rising air currents. This 'ballooning' of spiders (see Chapter 3) is inhibited by bad weather. When there is a thick covering of lines over the ground the sight has been described by W. S. Bristowe as a 'smother of spiders'. Many a poet and country-lover, such as Gilbert White, have also been inspired by the sight. Gossamer is an abbreviation of 'goose-summer', a special goose festival in England which is associated with fine weather in autumn.

In classical times it was an accepted fact of weather-forecasting that spiders' silk threads, drifting about in calm weather, were a sure sign of bad weather to come. Aristotle said it was because spiders were particularly active in calm weather. Pliny, on the other hand, said that spiders weave their webs in clear weather and then take them apart when bad weather comes

– thus it is the dismantled webs that float about in the air. He also said that the rising of rivers could be predicted by the sight of spiders setting their webs higher than usual, and he added that they can give forewarning of the imminent collapse of a building.

> Incey Wincey spider
> Climbing up the spout;
> Down came the rain
> And washed the spider out;
> Out came the sunshine
> And dried up all the rain;
> Incey Wincey spider
> Climbing up again.
>
> (MOTHER GOOSE)

THE STORIES
OF ANANSI THE SPIDER

The artfulness of spiders is greatly admired in West Africa. Anansi or Ananse the spider is the hero of many Ghanaian folk tales, having earned that role by outwitting God. These 'Spider Tales' came originally from the Hausa tribes and have since spread to America and the Caribbean – the stories are especially popular among children in Jamaica.

In the beginning, at God's command, a large black spider, called Anansi, spun the raw material out of which human beings were created. After he had spun enough for a multitude of humans he could do no more. But the people ran away without a word of thanks to the spider for all his trouble. Anansi, however, made one more man from the material that was left over. He was smaller than the previous lot and the spider brought him up himself and gave him his own name, Anansi.

Anansi was both spider and man. When things went well he was a man, but when in danger he became a spider, safe in his web high up on the ceiling. That was why he was also known as 'Ceiling Thomas'. When listening to the stories, children always laugh at the way he tricks the other animals and gets the better of those who are much bigger than himself. So when the children see a spider, they call him Ceiling Thomas. They know that he is Anansi, the spider man, and they do him no harm.

Anansi knew many tricks. He knew how to eat the flesh of the fowl and then put the bones and feathers back together again. He was also taught to suck the egg out through small holes in the shell, then refill the shell with sand, seal the holes, and sell it again for a high price in the market.

In a story related by P. M. Sherlock, Anansi and Moos-Moos the mouse were afraid of Kisander the cat, but they badly wanted one of the delicious puddings hanging on Kisander's dokanoo tree. So one night Anansi climbed the tree while Moos-Moos waited at the bottom. Carefully, Anansi crawled along a branch to a ripe pudding, which he cut causing it to fall 'boof' to the ground. Kisander heard the sound, and also a second 'boof', but only on the third 'boof' did he go out to see what was happening to his dokanoo tree. Moos-Moos shouted to Anansi, 'Ceiling Thomas, it's Kisander!' and then he ran off. Kisander saw the three puddings on the ground and took them back in the house. Anansi jumped from the tree – 'boof' and ran off. 'That's funny,' thought Kisander, 'there's no other pudding.' She never did find out what made that last 'boof'.

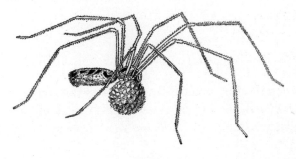

Poetry and Literature

Shakespeare was not a spider lover:

> Weaving spiders, come not here;
> Hence, you long-legg'd spinners, hence.
> *A Midsummer Night's Dream*, Act II, Scene II

He thought of them as full of venom:

> But let thy spiders, that suck up thy venom,
> And heavy-gaited toads, lie in their way.
> *King Richard II*, Act III, Scene II

From another passage, it seems that Shakespeare thought any injury a spider might cause, arose more from the imagination of the sufferer than the venom of the spider:

> There may be in the cup
> A spider steep'd, and one may drink, depart,
> And yet partake no venom, for his knowledge
> Is not infected; but if one present
> The abhorr'd ingredient to his eye, make known,
> How he hath drunk, he cracks his gorge, his sides,
> With violent hefts.
> *The Winter's Tale*, Act II, Scene I

On his mission to Ireland, St Patrick is said to have destroyed all vermin including spiders:

> Happy Ierne, whose most wholesome air
> Poisons envenomed spiders, and forbids
> The baleful toad and viper from her shore.

According to a Russian fable, a spider invited flies on to her web, ate most of them, and then pretended to be dead. The other insects rejoiced and fell on to the web of the spider, who ate them too.

[32]

Finally, the greatest poem in the English language on spiders:

> I have fought a grizzly bear,
> Tracked a cobra to its lair,
> Killed a crocodile who dared to cross my path;
> But the thing I really dread
> When I've just got out of bed
> Is to find that there's a spider in the bath.
>
> I've no fear of wasps or bees,
> Mosquitoes only tease,
> I rather like a cricket on the hearth;
> But my blood runs cold to meet
> In pyjamas and bare feet
> With a great big hairy spider in the bath.
>
> What a frightful-looking beast –
> Half an inch across at least –
> It would frighten even Superman or Garth.
> There's contempt it can't disguise
> In the little beady eyes
> Of the spider glowering in the bath.
>
> Now it's time for me to shave
> Though my nerves will not behave,
> And there's bound to be a fearful aftermath;
> So before I cut my throat
> I shall leave this final note:
> DRIVEN TO IT – BY THE SPIDER IN THE BATH!
>   (MICHAEL FLANDERS AND DONALD SWANN)

One may wonder – what did spiders do before there were baths?

Spiders in Art

Cave-painting of spider and flies

The earliest known representation of a spider is of a drawing on a cave wall by a prehistoric artist in Gasulla Gorge, Castellón, Spain. The spider appears to be fat in body and is accompanied by three flies. The ancient Incas, over 2,000 years ago at Nazca, Peru, etched enormous drawings of animals, birds and people in the desert sands. Their designs included a spider 160 feet (50 m) across, which only became apparent to modern man when he was able to fly over it. Today the origin and significance of the Nazca figures are steeped in mystery, and remain a puzzle to archaeologists.

The spider images and illustrations which survive from the medieval period have been researched by Paolo Tongiorgi of

Modena. He found that such images are unfortunately few in number, probably because of our inherent 'negative symbolism connected with the spider, emblem of the devil weaving his evil webs'. Nevertheless, one of the earliest surviving illustrations dates from the eleventh century. Its design is somewhat schematic and it is presently kept at the Abbey of Montecassino. According to Tongiorgi, splendid drawings of spiders in a fourteenth-century script from Genoa are preserved at the British Library. From the fifteenth century, a number of images of spiders and their webs appear in medical codices (preserved in the British Library; Vatican Apostolic Library; and Modena Estense Library).

The earliest images of spiders in printed books are those in the *Buch der Natur* (1475) by von Magenberg, and in the *Hortus Sanitatis* printed at Magonza (1491). In the latter, the best illustration is a spectacular representation of a spider on its orb-web. The first figures of spiders which may be described as realistic and reasonably scientific are those in *Die Animalibus Insectis* by Aldrovandus (1602) and *Insectorum Theatrum* by Mouffet (1634). The illuminated manuscripts on which they are based can be found today in the Bologna University Library and The British Library. Later in the seventeenth century, accurate images of spiders were used in 'herbals' (e.g. Ligozzi, Le Moyne de Morgues) and in 'notebooks on animals' (e.g. Hoefnagel) and in 'still-life' pictures (e.g. Bruegel de Velluti, Sniders). There are also spiders in an 'illuminated herbal' by the naturalistic painter Chellini (1672–1742), which is in the keeping of the Estense Library of Modena.

The Use of Spiders
in Medicine

Natural history and medicine have always been closely related. Many authors in history have been both physicians and naturalists – cures were derived from natural sources, whether herbal or animal, and thus a knowledge of the natural world was essential to a medical practitioner.

In classical times, spiders were used in the treatment of a variety of conditions. A kind of 'contraceptive cure', ascribed to Caecilius, used the phalangium spider: 'with a hairy body and head of enormous size . . . When cut open there are in it two small worms; these are to be attached before dawn in a piece of deer skin to a woman's body, when they will prevent conception but, for a year only.' According to Pliny, the cobwebs which line a spider's hole, applied to the forehead in a compress, would cure 'defluxions of the eyes'. In his *Theriaca* (published in French in 1568), Nicander, the ancient Greek, catalogued in a lurid manner the antidotes prescribed for bites from each of the phalangia (venomous spiders). He spared his readers none of the gruesome details. He prescribed rabbit curd, sheep dung, salt and red ochre, and advised treatment of the patient by immersion in wine, or by blood-letting with cupping glasses or leeches. Any bite victim who came to Nicander, ready to try anything once, would have surely ended up in a sorry plight.

In the sixteenth century, a great enthusiast was Dr Thomas Mouffet, or Muffet, mentioned in Chapter 1 for his habit of dosing his daughter Patience (who may have been the 'Little Miss Muffet' of the nursery rhyme) with spiders to cure her ailments. He said:

> ... for the most part I find those people to be free from Gowt in whose houses the spiders breed much. You may know there is nothing so filthy in a spider that is not good for something. The running of the eyes is stopped with the dung and urine of a House Spider dropt in with Oyl of Roses, or laid on alone with Wooll.

He went on to chide his fellow physicians for seeking exotic medications from the 'Indes', when one spider would do as much good as all their newly discovered drugs put together. Mouffet recorded several persons as having eaten spiders including, in England, 'a great lady still living who will not leave off eating them'.

WARDING-OFF FEVERS

There are many references in old European medical books to the prevention and cure of fevers, such as malaria (until its eradication there in the nineteenth century). Spiders were also useful in a number of conditions besides malaria – smallpox, plague, leprosy, gout, toothache, piles and headache. Furthermore, as a remedy for sexual impotence, spiders crushed into a powder were widely used during the Middle Ages and Renaissance.

In the sixteenth century, spiders hung in a bag or nutshell around the neck as amulets to ward off or draw out fevers, were advocated by many eminent men such as Matthiolus and Aldrovandus. However, the herbalist Gerade was sceptical, though he was, in effect, a competitor. In his *Historie of Plants*, he wrote: ' . . . spiders put in a nutshell and divers such foolish toies that I was constrained to take, did me no good at all'. On the other hand, Elias Ashmole the antiquarian, wrote in his diary for 11 May 1651: 'I took early in the morning a good dose of elixir, and hung three spiders about my neck. Ague away, Deo gratias'.

Eleazar Albin, the author of *A Natural History of Spiders and other curious Insects* (1736), asserted that he had cured many persons of stubborn malarial fevers. The medicine prescribed consisted of the web of the house spider mixed with mithridate. He added that he had cured several children of agues: 'by hanging a large spider, confined alive in a box, about their neck, reaching to the pit of their stomach, without giving any internal remedies'.

SPIDERS TAKEN INTERNALLY

If the medicine was actually swallowed, then the concentrated benefits could be gained. Swallowing spiders was, in theory, supposed to hasten the course of the fever by making the patient sweat. Other theories suggested that spiders and their webs contained arsenic, or that their effectiveness lay in their very *nastiness*, which made the sickness seem less bad by comparison. In western Kentucky, for the relief of constipation, it was believed that spiders should be eaten *in handfuls* on bread and butter. In Britain the species generally recommended was a house spider (*Tegenaria domestica*). Dr Mead, quoted by Sarah Harrison (1764) gave the following prescription:

> Take a spider alive, cover it with the new soft crummy bread without bruising it; let the patient swallow it fasting. This is an effectual cure, but many are set against it. It has been frequently given to people who did not know the contents and has had the desired effect.

Others, such as Dr Watson, in his *Lecture on Agues and Intermittent Fevers* (1760), preferred the following refinement: 'Swallow a spider gently bruised and wrapped up in a raison or spread upon bread and butter.' He claimed that spiders had been efficacious in more than sixty cases where the standard treatment of bark (Cinchona) had failed.

In Kentucky and other American States it was believed, until the last century, that you could cure a headache by swallowing a spider's web. In 1821, Nicholas Hentz wrote of the American *Coras medicinalis*, a spider related to *Tegenaria*: 'For some time the use of its web as a narcotic was recommended by many physicians in this country, but now is seldom used.' In 1890, interest in its medicinal value was said by Henry McCook to have been revived and he cited Dr Vinson's experience of becoming entangled in a huge web on the Indian Ocean island of Reunion: while detaching from his lips the sticky, bitter-tasting threads, Vinson predicted that they could be made into a medicine as a substitute for sulphate of quinine.

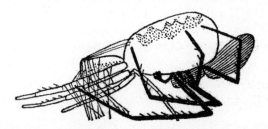

USING COBWEBS TO DRESS WOUNDS

The use of spiders' webs in staunching the flow of blood was advocated as early as the first century AD by Dioscorides. Later, in 1607, Topsell wrote that the cobweb 'binds, cooles, dries, glutinates, and will let no putrefaction continue long there!' Albin's prescription, a century later, was more detailed:

> The clean web of the house spider, dip it in the spawn of frogs, beaten as you would the white of eggs, several times

letting it dry on pewter and keep it in a box close stopped from air, and apply it when you have occasion. With this remedy I saved a gentleman of worth in Lincoln Inn Fields who had bled from the nose for several hours, when all applications failed which were used by two eminent surgeons.

Even today, the belief has persisted in some country areas that webs can be used to staunch blood flow and aid coagulation. It has been suggested that an enzyme which hardens the silk would also help to coagulate the blood. However, this is unlikely because the hardening of silk is a physical process which occurs as it emerges from the spinning organs. The second possible suggestion in a medical context is that the web might possess moulds, containing penicillin, which would thus have an antibiotic effect. But the reality is that a web, especially when old, is more likely to be a source of other contamination.

Both Ben Jonson and William Shakespeare mentioned the use of cobwebs to dress wounds. Bottom, addressing one of his fairy attendants, said:

I shall desire you of more acquaintance, good Master
    Cobweb.
If I cut my finger, I shall make bold with you.
SHAKESPEARE, *A Midsummer Night's Dream*, Act III, Scene I

He sweeps no cobwebs here, but sells 'em for cut fingers.
BEN JONSON, *The Staple of Newes*; a comedie

CHAPTER THREE

AERONAUTIC SPIDERS

After the most violent volcanic eruption in human history, that of Krakatoa in August 1883, the first scientist to set foot on the shattered island, in May 1884, reported:

> Notwithstanding all my searches, I was unable to observe any symptoms of animal life. I only discovered one microscopic spider – only one; this strange pioneer of the renovation was busy spinning its web.

Only one? No matter! That solitary spider was evidence enough of their ability, in spite of having no wings, to cross at least 25 miles of sea and to arrive on virgin territory *before* the flying insects. In fact they even have time to build their webs and wait!

Their method is to sail through the air. Small spiders attached to lines of silk often occur in considerable numbers high above the earth's surface. This unique method of aeronautic dispersal is known as *ballooning*. It is an effective means for small spiders, which normally lie concealed in vegetation, and young ones, which have just hatched in their hundreds from an egg sac, to spread out and colonise new lands. But for the individual aeronaut it is a risky adventure. When spiders attached to lines of silk achieve lift-off, the breeze becomes their master and they may be carried to any destination. For all those that make a fortunate landing, probably many more are deposited in unsuitable places or even far out at sea.

Spider ballooning may occur almost anywhere and at any time of the year, unless it is actually freezing. It is particularly

Watching spiders ballooning

noticeable in late summer and autumn, especially during clear weather when the breezes are gentle. In woods, fields, moors and heaths, on pleasant sunny mornings, a multitude of silk lines may be seen floating on the air and gleaming in the sun. Later, during the afternoon, when the air is no longer rising, spiders can be found landing on people's clothes or in their hair. Towards evening, whole fields may become covered by a carpet of silk.

OBSERVATIONS IN HISTORICAL TIMES

The Ancient Greeks were aware that spiders could float on the air, but the exact mechanism remained for long the subject of speculation. Aristotle thought that the spider could shoot out silk in the manner of the porcupine its quills (according to the belief of his time). Other explanations, which remained popular until the seventeenth century, were that spiders' threads had less specific gravity than air and therefore gave lift; or that air–sacs were inflated within their bodies to reduce the specific gravity; or that they could swim in the air by means of a rapid vibration of their eight legs. It was even suggested that spiders might be assisted by electricity.

In 1668, a lively debate arose in Britain on the subject of ballooning. Dismissing the theories of the Ancient Greeks, John Ray (see page 148) rejected those 'vulgar Philosophizers' who 'invented such awkward and ridiculous causes' and, in their place, he sought an explanation from Martin Lister (see page 148), who undoubtedly understood the phenomenon. But Lister was also somewhat speculative, he wrote:

I have ascertained for sure that *Spiders exercise the power of flight*, not only for pleasure but also to catch gnats and other tiny creatures, with which the air is filled in incredible numbers in autumn.

A SPIDER BECOMES AIRBORNE

Given the right time and place it is possible to observe what actually happens during an embarkation. The spider climbs to the top of a fence post or other prominent point. It turns to face the wind and stands on 'tip-toes'. The abdomen is elevated to an angle of about 45 degrees and, from the spinnerets at the end of the abdomen, a line of silk is drawn out by the breeze. When the upward lift on the line is sufficient, the spider swivels round, grabs the thread with its legs, releases its hold on the post, and away it goes. On days when the air is calm, however, some spiders first drop down on a thread and then climb back up again. This adds a loop to their line which can then be said to rise on the air like a 'balloon'. The process was described by J. S. Phillpotts:

> Lying in my hot bath one evening, I noticed a tiny spider on the hot tap. It lost its footing, fell a few inches, recovered itself and to my relief climbed back to the tap. But, horrors, it fell again and again till it had miraculously saved itself from death five or six times. Then, having apparently cut all its loops of web loose, and holding on to this little parachute, it floated up with the steam, to the ceiling and safety!

Some people, having watched spiders become airborne, have tried to follow them and discover how high and far they travel. The earliest observation is by Martin Lister (1670):

> As to the height that they are able to mount, it is much beyond that of trees or even the highest steeples in England. This last October the sky here upon a day was very calm and serene and I took notice that the air was very full of webs. I forthwith mounted to the top of the highest steeple in the Minster [York] and could then discern them exceeding high above me.

The reality that spiders can and do make arrivals in large numbers after travelling considerable distances by air was first attested to by Charles Darwin in the *Voyage of the Beagle*. He recorded that on 1 November 1832, at a distance of 60 miles (96 km) from the coast of South America, when sailing before a steady light breeze, the rigging became covered with vast numbers of dusky red spiders about one-tenth of an inch (2.55 mm) in length. Naming this the 'gossamer spider', Darwin encountered it again on the 25th, in similar circumstances. He was either very lucky with his sightings or they suggest that such a fall of spiders at sea is not a rare event.

The presence of tiny spiders as high as 14,000 feet (4,500 m) (though most are below 200 feet (60 m)) has been confirmed in recent years in collections made by aircraft flying over Europe and North America. In 1965, researchers collected spiders, in small numbers, on a ship in the Pacific Ocean, one thousand miles from the nearest land (Hawaii).

THE PHENOMENON OF GOSSAMER

The occurrence of gossamer is connected with ballooning but the two should not be confused. On days when there is much ballooning activity, either taking-off or landing, there can be more than a million spiders to the acre, each one trailing a line wherever it goes. Lines may thus accumulate to form a silvery sheet which, on a sunny, dewy morning, makes a beautiful sight. But, as the morning progresses and the dew is evaporated, rising air currents break up the sheet and lift the resulting pieces of gossamer into the air. While these might seem to be 'aeronauts' 'parachutes', they are not in fact ridden by spiders.

In English, the word gossamer derives from *goose-summer*. In France gossamer is known as *fils de la Vierge*; in Germany as *Altweibersommer* or *Marienfaden* ('Our Lady's threads'); and in

Japan as *yukimukae* (ushering in snow). 'Gossamer events' seem rarely these days to reach the epic proportions of earlier times. The Reverend Gilbert White in the *Natural History of Selborne* described a notable occurrence in England on 21 September 1741. He wrote:

> At daybreak I found the stubbles and clover grounds matted all over with a thick coat of cobweb, in the meshes of which a copious and heavy dew hung so plentifully that the whole face of the country seemed, as it were, covered with two or three nets drawn one over the other. When the dogs attempted to hunt, their eyes were so blinded and hood-winked that they could not proceed, but were obliged to lie down and scrape the incumbrances from their faces with their fore-feet, so that, finding my sport interrupted, I returned home musing in my mind on the oddness of the occurrence.

Later in the morning as the sun became bright and warm:

> An appearance very unusual began to demand our attention, a shower of cobwebs falling from very elevated regions and continuing, without any interruption, till the close of day. These webs were not single filmy threads, floating in the air, but perfect flakes or rags; some near an inch broad, and five or six long, which fell with a degree of velocity that showed they were considerably heavier than the atmosphere. On every side as the observer turned his eyes might he behold a continual succession of fresh flakes falling into his sight, and twinkling like stars as they turned their sides towards the sun.

According to Dr Willis Gertsch, places in California, such as in the Yosemite Valley, act as natural traps for spider threads carried on the wind. Here the leaves of bushes and trees become thickly covered with sheets of cotton-like material. In a gentle breeze the white-decked vegetation moves with a graceful, undulating motion, but in rougher weather the gossamer is broken up and drifts away to return to earth later, probably somewhere else in the State. In France, W. S. Bristowe recorded one remarkable warm, sunny day during the Second World War when a gossamer shower resembling snow-flakes descended and caused considerable anxiety, until an analysis proved that it was not a new form of chemical warfare!

CONTINUED RESEARCH

The mechanism of ballooning is not yet completely understood. Even the way spiders initially send forth their thread remains uncertain, though it is unlikely that they 'squeeze' the silk out. Many observations on ballooning spiders have been made through the use of wind tunnels. In fact small spiders can be encouraged to take off from a finger if one blows steadily at them – they tilt their abdomens and rise into the air.

A number of intriguing questions remain to be fully answered: for example, can spiders have any control over the duration of their flight? Theoretically, yes, because they can shorten the thread by rolling it up to cause a more rapid descent. In fact, it has been discovered that spiders can adjust their speed of fall by changing their posture – they descend more quickly if the legs are drawn in than if the legs are extended and waving about. And what about the use of extra lift? Could spiders fly *farther* by building 'sails' into the thread, as suggested by some observations? Well, yes, it seems so. As far back as 1668, Lister remarked:

> while they are flying along, their front legs whirling rapidly around, they haul back to themselves the whole of this very long thread and wind it into a ball or loops, constantly replenishing and releasing new threads for their flight.

Probably it is true that spiders have little or no control over their direction of flight. But what if they do land in an unsuitable place – might they decide to take off again? Yes, this certainly happens on ships at sea; Darwin observed it many times on the *Beagle*. In fact it is now firmly established that spiders will move on again if they find themselves in a poor situation. Their 'decision' may be influenced by factors such as: competition for space and food; adverse temperatures and humidity; excessive predation; and disturbance – by wind, rain, animals or humans. But how long the spider takes to judge the quality of a site is another question.

Surveys of precisely what kinds of spiders indulge in aeronautic dispersal have continued since J. H. Emerton listed 69 species of spiders in the aerial fauna over Massachusetts in the autumn of 1918. Broadly speaking there are two categories: the young, recently hatched spiders of many different species; and the adults (and young) of the family of 'money spiders' (Linyphiidae), all of which are less than the size of a pea – 25 mg is approximately the upper weight limit for ballooning. During a survey of species begun in Britain in the 1980s, one of the best contributions came from a primary school in Surrey. They sent a live sample of ballooners; the package was opened and, when the lid was lifted, the spiders attempted to take off and continue on their journeys!

> A lover may bestride the gossamer
> That idles in the wanton summer air,
> And yet not fall; so light is vanity.
> SHAKESPEARE, *Romeo and Juliet*, Act II, Scene VI

CHAPTER FOUR

VENOMOUS
SPIDERS

SPIDER BITE HORROR

Huge, poisonous spiders are invading the town of
Antofagasta. They are attacking the inhabitants. Their bite
inflicts great wounds like the gash of a knife. Twenty
persons, including nine children, are already in hospital
suffering from such wounds. Nothing like these spiders has,
apparently, ever been seen before. They are of an unknown
species. An 'SOS' has been received by the public health
authorities in Santiago, Chile from doctors declaring
themselves powerless in the face of this invasion . . . 'Large
and black' is the further brief telegraphic description.

Thus ran a vivid newspaper report from Reuters Agency in
April 1934. More realistic reports have come from medical
sources in the United States. For example, the case of a 55-year-
old Californian physician who was bitten by a 'black widow
spider':

The creature came from beneath the seat of a privy and bit
him three times on the testicles. Fiery, excruciating pain
followed, and the stomach muscles became as stiff as a
board. The physician diagnosed his own case and decided
upon the treatment. Unfortunately, antiseptics and narcotics
were powerless to relieve the pain and complications
ensued. He lost his appetite, suffered paralysis from a

stroke, because of raised blood pressure, and finally died from a diseased appendix and peritonitis.

Another case told of a 15-year-old girl who took straws from a hay stack during warm weather on Rhode Island:

> As she did so, a black spider with 'very shiny eyes' ran on to the back of her hand. That afternoon the affected hand, as well as the arm, began to twitch and pain. The pain gradually shifted to her stomach, increasing in intensity until the mid morning of the third day when she became hysterical. She was vomiting and a physician was called. He treated her for nothing more than hysteria but despite that she subsequently recovered.

She was fortunate.

THE OCCURRENCE OF VENOMOUS SPIDERS

Early human cultures probably thought of venomous creatures as a kind of punishment meted out by evil gods. In the past, snakes and scorpions were undoubtedly feared more than spiders. But today, as snakes become less common, and venomous scorpions are relatively localised in their distribution, only spiders can be said to be thriving alongside man. And, as luck would have it, the kinds of spiders which adapt readily to man-made environments tend to include the poisonous or, more correctly, venomous species. (Venomous means delivering or injecting venom; poisonous means toxic.)

In Chile, a country where venomous snakes are virtually absent, fatalities caused by spider bites are by no means unknown. In southern California, as many as 400 spider bites are reported to doctors each year; most of the victims are children or farm labourers working in the fruit plantations. In Brazil, in the region of São Paulo and Rio de Janeiro, approximately 45 per cent of the accidents from venomous or poisonous creatures are the result of spider bites. One hospital in São Paulo treated 1,136 spider bites in 1983; 60 per cent of the bites were caused by the much feared 'Brazilian wandering spider' (*Phoneutria nigriventer*). Even in a country like Great Britain, where the chance of meeting a dangerous spider is slim, the risk is nevertheless increasing because of introductions from abroad.

MUCH-FEARED SPIDERS

'Brazilian wandering spiders', which have a leg span of about five inches (12 cm), are common in urban areas where they find shelter and abundant food (cockroaches and other insects). They live beneath fallen trees, in piles of wood, in the midst of building rubble, in banana bunches and bromeliads. They hunt actively at night and rapidly overcome their prey with the strength of their venom; they do not construct webs. Often wandering spiders will enter houses, where they find hiding places during the day such as in shoes and under furniture and doorknobs. The spider is aggressive to humans and, in contrast to other species, does not retreat when molested. It can leap on to, and climb rapidly up, the handle of a broom used to fend it off. For defence, it may adopt a threatening posture by opening its red-coloured jaws and raising the first two pairs of legs. The bite of the spider causes immediate and intense pain which spreads throughout the whole body. At greatest risk are children because they are likely to be slow to take avoiding action. Their smaller body mass also makes them more susceptible to the effects of the bite.

Unlike the 'Brazilian wandering spider', many spiders whose bites are dangerous are actually timid and quite unimpressive. Perhaps the best example is the 'black widow spider'. When disturbed, black widows often let themselves fall

[51]

THE BOOK OF THE SPIDER

from their web and pretend to be dead. Usually they bite only when accidentally pressed against the body of the victim. However, the bite can be extremely painful, not so much at the actual site of penetration than in the chest, lower abdomen and legs. Many muscles go into spasm or cramp. The pain has been described as being similar to having one's flesh torn away by a pack of wild dogs. It is said that patients who had previously suffered from painful illnesses or operations, or difficult birth deliveries, would usually claim that they were tolerable in comparison with the agony of a black widow spider bite.

In medical terms, the symptoms of black widow spider bites are *systemic*, with accelerated heart beat, increased blood pressure, breathing difficulties and muscle paralysis. If death does occur it is usually because the breathing muscles are paralysed and the victim suffocates. Black widow venom is claimed to be fifteen times more potent than that of a rattlesnake. However, because the quantity injected is so minute, the mortality of untreated victims is no more than 5 per cent compared with the 15 to 20 per cent in the cases of rattlesnake bite.

THE POISONED KISS

Spiders employ venom to immobilise prey and for defence. Because they use their jaws, or chelicerae, spiders *bite*, whereas scorpions, bees and wasps have a *sting* in their tail. A victim may feel the venom's effects at the site of the bite (locally), or throughout the body (systemic), or as a combination of both. By contrast, the stings of bees, wasps and ants are essentially local in their effect unless the number of stings is very great. In the act of biting, the spider's fangs are jabbed into the skin and held there for up to several seconds while the venom glands are squeezed by muscles to deliver the toxic liquid via ducts which

open at the ends of the fangs. A spider bite can be distinguished from an insect sting by its double puncture mark.

With the notable exception of one family of spiders which lacks venom glands (the Uloboridae), all spiders are venomous – if not always for man then at least for insects, their usual prey. Most are harmless to humans. Of the close on 35,000 known species of spiders in the world, perhaps 500 or so are capable of inflicting a significant bite on man. But when it comes to finding and identifying the culprit, there is invariably a difficulty of diagnosis. The question of identity is important because different species of spiders have venoms with different chemical compositions causing, in turn, a variety of clinical symptoms requiring different medical treatment. Furthermore, spiders tend to get the blame for assorted bites and stings from other creatures such as scorpions, ticks, kissing bugs, bed bugs and fleas. And, besides the difficulties of identification, there are few areas in the medical world which are so entangled with old beliefs and superstitions.

It is interesting to speculate on the relative importance of venom and silk in the evolutionary success of the Order. In contrast to scorpions and other Arachnida, spiders lack features such as grasping claws to help subdue prey. Their chelicerae are relatively small and their bodies are soft and easily injured. Thus the ability of spiders to stop prey and opponents quickly, by snagging them in a web or with a venomous bite, is of critical importance. Some, such as the 'Brazilian wandering spider', depend particularly on a fast-acting venom while others rely more on constructing elaborate webs. Some, such as the black widow spider, have complicated webs *and* potent venom.

The Story of Tarantism

The longest and most famous epidemic of spider bites occurred in Italy during the Middle Ages. By all accounts the country was gripped in a kind of mania for over 300 years. According to Pietro Matthiole of Siena, it was near the town of Taranto in southern Italy that the first case of tarantism was recorded in 1370. The species of spider which was alleged to cause the bites was the original tarantula (*Lycosa tarantula*). The victims, the *tarantati*, sought relief from the bites by doing the *tarantella*, a lively dance which was supposed to flush the venom from the body. The symptoms suffered by the *tarantati* were said to include severe pain and swelling, muscle spasms, vomiting, palpitation, fainting, priapism (involuntary erections), shameless exhibitionism, acute melancholia and delirium, leading to death if untreated. Apparently, the victims died either laughing or crying. Unfortunately the drugs of the time were of no use and even alcoholic intoxication could not bring relief. The only cure was music and dancing which had to be prolonged and strenuous, resulting in copious sweating.

Samuel Pepys was intrigued by these strange events and he mentioned tarantism and the musical cure in his Diary (1662). He wrote that a Mr Templar, a great traveller, had informed him that 'all harvest long there are fiddlers who go up and down the fields everywhere in expectation of being hired by those who are stung'. Victims were offered a choice of tune. But different writers on the subject were for many years unable to agree on whether the whole thing was true or false. Descriptions of authenticated cases of tarantism alternated with equally confident denials that the attacks were anything more than midsummer madness or mass hysteria. A Neapolitan physician, Dr Thomas Cornelius, wrote in 1672 that the *tarantati* were either malingerers, wanton young women or half-wits. He

THE BOOK OF THE SPIDER

added that many people, especially women, simulated being bitten and then danced and raved under the pretext.

THE SPIDER IS INVESTIGATED

In 1695, Georges Baglivi, an eminent Italian physician, was the first respected academic to accurately describe and illustrate the spider, *Lycosa tarantula*. He was confident that tarantism was a true clinical condition resulting from the bite of this particular spider. Indeed, his description of the symptoms was highly credible. He discussed the treatment, and noted the greater frequency of the disease in the month of July. Georges Baglivi distinguished 'true' from 'pretended' tarantism and he also mentioned some different kinds of tarantula, for example the black 'uvea' which had the appearance of a grape. However, he mistakenly said that the spider dies soon after biting the victim.

Dr Richard Mead, who was interested in poisons, wrote in 1736:

> the bite of the tarantula is harmless in winter but in the dog days of summer the victims are seized by a violent sickness and they dance for three or four hours, then rest, continuing for three or four days by which time they are generally freed from all their symptoms, which do nevertheless attack them about the same time the next year.

Dr Mead commented that the affected, or *tarantati*, while dancing, 'talk and act obscenely, and take great pleasure in playing with leaves and swords'.

Oliver Goldsmith recorded in *An History of the Earth and Animated Nature* (1795), that while visiting Italy he attended the dances and, for scientific reasons, caused a servant to be bitten by a *Lycosa tarantula*. There was no serious result; nothing more than a slight swelling and discoloration at the site of the bite with intense itching. Since then, many other medical scientists carried out tests which came to discredit the belief that *Lycosa tarantula* could possibly have caused great suffering to masses of people in Europe. Their observations repeatedly found that no serious result ensued from the bite of this spider.

However, there can be no doubt that the dances did actually occur; indeed they are part of history. So if the spider was not really to blame then the most likely explanation is that the dances were in effect an antidote to the bleak conditions of life which followed in the wake of the Black Death. It was a period when superstition, ignorance, repression, war and disease all contributed to fear and insecurity. And with the coming of Christianity, orgies were banned. Thus the 'choreomania' of tarantism, indulged in every summer, gave the people just the excuse they needed to relieve all their neuroses, frustrations, monotony and nymphomania!

Having possessed Italy, where it was at its height in the seventeenth century, the mania spread to southern France, Spain, Istria and Dalmatia. By the late eighteenth century the mass hysteria was in decline, though the *tarantella* remained popular and still is so in Italy. Even today, pockets of tarantism are said to have survived in some remote parts of Spain, southern Italy and Sardinia. In Sardinia, tarantism was known as *Arza* but was claimed to be always caused by real bites, unlike the more institutionalised tarantism in southern Italy. In Sardinia, the local cure involved putting the poor victim into a refuse-heap up to his neck. If a man, he would be surrounded by seven women dancing around the dung heap as exorcists. If he laughed, that was a sign of recovery; if he couldn't laugh, he would die.

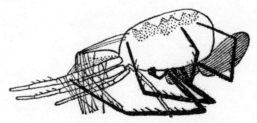

THE REAL CULPRIT

Today, after examining all the evidence, it seems that a spider was actually part of the story but that the wrong species had been blamed. Thus the real culprit was not *Lycosa tarantula*, recognised today as a kind of wolf spider, but in fact *Latrodectus tredecimguttatus* – the Mediterranean equivalent of the black widow, known in parts of southern Europe as the 'malmignatte'. The symptoms which had been described were therefore accurate in terms of the malmignatte, the bite of which has a systemic effect on the whole body of the victim. Furthermore, the malmignatte has always occurred in southern Italy. It can be abundant in the fields but this spider is shy and less obvious than the larger *Lycosa tarantula*. Probably when the harvesters were looking for a culprit they found the wrong species. Of course, the study of spiders and the identification of the different kinds was then in its infancy. Georges Baglivi had been close to the truth when he described the different 'varieties' of tarantula – his 'uvea' was undoubtedly the malmignatte.

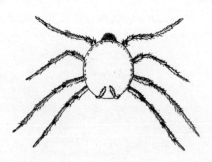

Types of Venomous Spiders

THE BLACK WIDOWS

The black widow of North America, the malmignatte of southern Europe, the araña brava of Chile, the araña del lino of Argentina, the araña capulina of Mexico, the red-back of Australia, the katipo of New Zealand, and the button spider of South Africa are all closely related examples of the thirty or so species which belong to the worldwide genus *Latrodectus*. Their distribution is in those parts of the world where grapes grow. None of them is larger than a thumbnail, and mostly their appearance is globular, resembling a grape, shiny black and red (i.e. the females, the males are tiny and do not bite).

In the USA the black widow (*Latrodectus mactans*) accounts for about 50 per cent of the total spider bites, though many go unrecorded. This spider is most abundant in California where the number of recorded cases during the period 1726 and 1943 (before the availability of an antivenom) was 578 with 32 deaths. More than 80 per cent of the victims were males. Nowadays, deaths are much less frequent. But in nineteenth-century America there were many tales of extreme fear concerning the effects of black widow spider bites. One story, related by Charlotte Taylor (1860), was that of a man 'stung' by a black widow while out hunting. Following the bite, he gave away his watch, bade his friends goodbye, and made preparations for an early demise.

During the early years of colonisation in North America, the medical profession was unfamiliar with the symptoms of spider bites. On the frontier, many bites were wrongly diagnosed and sometimes unnecessary operations were performed. For example, black widow spider bites often cause abdominal rigidity but this was frequently misdiagnosed as a perforated appendix, or peritonitis. The first serious medical investigation into spider bites in the USA was published in 1889 by Riley and Howard. Their book reflected the general scientific opinion at the time which doubted the existence in the USA of any spider which could possibly cause dire effects in a healthy body. But Dr C. R. Corson was one of many other physicians who responded that spiders of the genus *Latrodectus* were indeed very poisonous and that their bites had been followed by severe illnesses and, in some cases, death. He said that this spider had a venom which, considering its size and the quantity of the poison, exceeded that of any other living thing – at least when administered in tender parts of the body. He pointed out that the spider inhabited privies which in those days were commonly outdoors. Consequently, the site of the bite in a goodly proportion of the male patients was on the penis. What seemed to happen in these cases was that the spider was attracted to the vibration caused by a stream of water splashing on the web.

In an extensive collection of spider bite cases, Dr Browning (1901) recorded that on 26 July 1900 at Fullerton, California, Dr Clark attended a patient who had been bitten on the penis by a spider in an outhouse and who was suffering great pain at the site of the bite. The doctor's examination revealed two tiny pink spots on the glans. Severe pain and muscle spasms developed in the victim's abdomen, legs and back, and there was difficulty in breathing, with perspiration, vomiting, a temperature of 105 degrees, restlessness and delirium. In his suffering, the patient would throw himself on to the bed, then into a chair, and then roll on the floor, over and over again. From the start he seemed to be possessed with the idea that he was fatally bitten and would inevitably die. In fact, death did occur approximately 13 hours after the bite despite various treatments. The next day the water closet was opened up to reveal three or four shiny black, medium-sized spiders with red spots.

The American arachnologist, Dr Baerg, of Fayetteville, Arkansas, made a brave gesture to scientific accuracy when in

1922 he arranged for himself to be bitten by a black widow. He survived the bite but suffered considerably and reported later:

> The first test proved very difficult and ended in failure; it is not always easy to make the black widow bite. The second test resulted in all I could wish. The spider dug into the third finger of the left hand and held on till I removed her about 5 or 6 seconds later. The pain at first was faint but very soon began to increase into a sharp piercing sensation. In less than one hour the pain had reached the shoulder and within two hours the chest was affected; the diaphragm seemed partially paralysed, breathing and speech became spasmodic. After 5 hours the pain extended to the legs and after 9 hours I was taken to hospital. A severe nausea and excruciating pain not only kept me awake but kept me moving throughout the night. In the morning I took a hot bath and found the pain somewhat relieved. The pain in lesser degree returned after the bath and in the evening I was able to eat but the following night my sleep was much disturbed by unpleasant dreams. I left the hospital after three days but found that recovery was not complete; a feeling of wretchedness remained for a couple of days.

CLASSES OF VENOM

Spider venoms and their effect on man may be divided into two basic classes: neurotoxic, affecting the nervous system, and cytotoxic or necrotic, causing damage to the tissues. Some venoms may have both effects. Spider venoms are complex mixtures containing particular toxic components. For example, the principal toxic component of black widow venom is *a-latrotoxin*. It is a large protein with a molecular weight of about 130,000. Low molecular weight proteins are found among some other spiders such as the Australian funnelwebs. The syndrome resulting from a spider bite (envenomation) is termed araneism or, in the particular case of a black widow bite, latrodectism. Envenomation may affect a large part of the body and can last for a number of days depending on factors such as quantity delivered, rate of absorption, accumulation of toxin at the receptor sites, metabolism and excretion.

NEUROTOXIC VENOMS

The black widow (*Latrodectus*) is the best known example of a spider with a neurotoxic venom. The venom acts to block the transmission of nerve impulses to the muscles, causing rigidity and cramp. It over-stimulates the transmitters acetylcholine and noradrenalin, causing paralysis of both the sympathetic and parasympathetic nervous systems. The combined effect is to impose a sudden and severe stress on the human body. But the effects differ on other animals. Tests have discovered that the cat is very susceptible to the venom while dogs are quite resistant and high doses are necessary to cause death. In the case of sheep and rabbits, these animals are almost entirely resistant. By contrast, some large animals are very susceptible. Venom extracted from one black widow caused the death of a horse while the injection of a preparation from a macerated black widow killed a large camel (thus *Latrodectus* is both venomous and poisonous). In insects, which are the regular prey of *Latrodectus*, the venom causes rapid paralysis which prevents escape or retaliation; the spider begins to suck the body juices while the prey is still alive.

NECROTIC VENOMS

Necrotic venoms cause skin blisters which may lead to ulcers and the blackening of the tissues (necrosis) around the site of the bite. This category of venom, containing high molecular weight proteins, occurs also in some snakes (e.g. vipers). Scorpions, and most other snakes, possess venoms which are predominantly neurotoxic in action. In general terms, neurotoxic venoms kill more quickly than necrotic venoms.

The 'recluse spiders' (*Loxosceles*) are the best known and most poisonous of the spiders which possess a necrotic venom. The necrosis they cause (loxoscelism) may heal slowly or not at all. Worldwide there are about 50 species of 'recluse spiders' but the most important are: *Loxosceles laeta* (South and Central America), *L.gaucho* (Brazil), *L.reclusa* (southern USA), and *L.rufescens* (cosmopolitan, including USA, Japan, Australia and Europe). They are small to medium sized, very ordinary-looking spiders, brown in colour. In many countries they inhabit houses and, in their nocturnal movements, they often crawl into clothes and bedding. Most victims are bitten when sleeping or dressing. It is reported that *L.laeta* infests 30–40 per cent of buildings in Chile, where it is known as the *araña de los rincones* ('corner spider') or the *araña de detras de los cuadros* ('spider behind the pictures'). The first symptom following a bite, 20 per cent of which occur on the face, is usually a local, burning-stinging sensation. Additionally, most patients experience restlessness, vomiting and general malaise. There are two form of loxoscelism; a cutaneous, non life-threatening form; and a dangerous, life-threatening form which affects the kidneys, causing the urine to turn black. In Peru, during the period 1962 to 1976, 110 cases of 'recluse spider' bite were recorded, with 12 deaths. In the United States during 1896 to 1968 there were 126 cases, with 6 deaths. Loxoscelism is said to be next to latrodectism as the most important form of araneism in the USA.[1]

A most horrifying case, widely reported in 1993, was that of a housewife living near Los Angeles. She ended up having both arms and legs and the tip of her nose amputated. The initial bite, diagnosed as that of a 'recluse spider', caused an extreme allergic reaction and she fell into a coma after developing toxic shock syndrome. She awoke five months later, by which time gangrene had affected all her extremities.

In South America, the bite of some wolf spiders, e.g. *Lycosa raptoria* and *erythrognatha*, relatives of the European *Lycosa tarantula*, are known to cause a deep, gangrenous necrosis. Following the bite, a swollen area up to a foot across usually develops after three or four days into an ulcerous necrosis, which later becomes a large permanent scar.

In many countries araneism is most likely to be caused by spiders of the genus *Chiracanthium* ('running spiders'). Their bite causes a characteristically yellow inflammation and sometimes a mild necrosis. *Chiracanthium* is a pale, insignificant-looking spider which is represented in most regions of the world by venomous species: *C. japonicum* (Japan), *C. lawrencei* (South Africa), *C. diversum* (Australia), *C. punctorium* (Europe), *C. inclusum* (USA), and *C. mildei* (USA and Europe). In South Africa, *Sicarius hahnii*, buries itself in sand but is said to be among the most toxic of all spiders. It is a relative of *Loxosceles* but fortunately is not aggressive and rarely bites man – the bite can lead to an extensive necrosis and secondary infection.

---

[1] Dr Findlay Russell of Arizona has pointed out that many bites blamed on *Loxosceles* are actually caused by a host of other antagonists, including 'kissing bugs', 'pajaroello ticks', other spiders such as *Chiracanthium* and *Steatoda*, poison ivy, bed sores, allergic reactions, and even stress reactions. Another possible cause of necrosis may be the one presently suspected in Australia – where a mysterious necrotic sore, which sometimes follows bites of the common 'white-tailed spider' (*Lampona cylindrata*), is at the centre of a debate between doctors and museum arachnologists (Raven). The culprit may turn out to be a bacterium (*Mycobacterium*) which infects the mouthparts of the spider.

Venomous Spiders Around the World

TARANTULAS OR BIRD-EATING SPIDERS

South America is probably the continent which has the greatest number of venomous spiders. It is also the headquarters of the large hairy spiders of the family Theraphosidae, popularly known, among English-speakers, as *tarantulas* (the name was usurped from the Italian wolf spider *Lycosa tarantula*). In Britain they used to be called *bird-eating spiders*; in Germany they are *Vogelspinnen*, in France *mygale* and in parts of Latin America *mata-caballos*. Because they look so 'horrible', they have always been imagined to be dangerous or even fatally venomous.

The celebrated Dr Baerg (1958) did his best to answer the question: How poisonous are tarantulas? He used rats and guinea pigs to test the bites of 26 species. The common 'Trinidadian tarantula' (*Avicularia velutina*) he described as: 'extremely pugnacious in attitude and it at first impressed me as probably venomous. When I tried to place it in position to bite a white rat, it bit instead the third finger of my right hand. However, the effects of the poison turned out to be harmless.' Baerg found that only the 'Panamanian tarantula' (*Sericopelma communis*) could be described as venomous. Tested on himself, it bit a finger which 'became swollen and very painful within 15 minutes. After putting the hand in hot water for 20 minutes, the finger bent more easily but continued to be painful. However, the effects remained local and disappeared at the end of the following day.' Baerg concluded that South American tarantulas are not seriously venomous, the bite of most species being no more painful than a pair of pin pricks. In all tarantulas the venom glands are small and lie inside the chelicerae. In most other spiders the glands are relatively larger, reaching far into the

[65]

cephalothorax. Baerg suggested that tarantula venom is intended only to assist in the digestion of prey. However, other investigators have found that some genera (e.g. *Pamphobeteus, Acanthoscurria, Theraphosa* and *Phormictopus*) should be accorded respect because of the paralysis and necrosis they can cause in laboratory animals.

The tarantulas or 'baboon spiders' (family Theraphosidae) of Africa have quite a fearsome reputation. Invariably, native Africans believe that a bite will be fatal though no doctor is known to have recorded any deaths. In West Africa, the large 'pigeon spiders', *Stromatopelma* and *Heteroscodra*, are reported by Philip Charpentier to be capable of giving very painful bites: 'while climbing a palm tree I was bitten below the little finger of the left hand by a large female [*Heteroscodra*]. While dropping from the tree, the spider ran up my arm and jumped away – unfortunately upon the chest of my African guide and bit him on the left pectoral muscle. The bite is similar to *Stromatopelma* bites with intense and immediate pain. It stabilized in one and a quarter hours and subsequently decreased. The lymph nodes in my left armpit were extremely painful for 24 hours. My African guide was even more unfortunate, with agonizing pain spreading through the whole thoracic part, down the abdomen with apparently excruciating pain in the lymph nodes and groin.' Some other genera in Africa are also venomous: e.g. *Hysterocrates* and *Phoneyusa*. In India and Sri Lanka the most venomous genus is *Poecilotheria*; in South–East Asia and Australia, the most venomous is probably *Selenocosmia*.

AUSTRALIAN FUNNELWEB SPIDERS

In Australia there are many venomous spiders, perhaps as many as 50 to 100 species. The two best known of the medically important spiders are the 'red-back' (*Latrodectus hasselti*) and the 'Sydney funnelweb spider' (*Atrax robustus*). Both have caused deaths but none has been caused by red-backs since the development of an antivenom. The Sydney funnelweb spider is commonly found in the suburbs of Sydney and, quite unusually among spiders, it is the males that cause most of the bites. Drops of venom appear at the tips of the large fangs and the spider strikes repeatedly and furiously at anything that moves. The fangs can even penetrate the skull of a small animal or human finger nail. If the fangs are embedded, it is difficult to remove the spider, especially from a child's finger nail. Needless to say, the bite is very painful, partly because of the depth of penetration and partly because the venom is highly acidic.

The venom of the Sydney funnelweb spider is neurotoxic and systemic effects begin within ten minutes – nausea and vomiting, abdominal pain, excessive fluid production, sweating, salivation, lacrimation and an accumulation of fluid in the lungs. Paralysis does not occur but muscle twitching can be intense. The patient may sink into a coma, with the accompanying risk of asphyxiation and cardiac arrest. In three cases of infant mortality, the victims died within 15 to 90 minutes of being bitten. Thus the prompt application of a tourniquet may be a life-saver. Adult victims, however, can take more than 30 hours to die. The properties of the principal toxic component, atraxotoxin (10 per cent by volume), are somewhat puzzling. It is known to be made up of proteins with low molecular weight but the noxious effects of atraxotoxin are seen only in man and monkey; other animals seem to be less susceptible.

EUROPEAN VENOMOUS SPIDERS

Europe has its share of spiders which are capable of biting humans but, *Latrodectus* apart, fatalities are virtually unknown. In western Europe, significant bites are most likely to be caused by: the 'woodlouse spider' (*Dysdera crocata*), the 'tube spider' (*Segestria florentina*), the 'mouse spider' (*Scotophaeus blackwalli*), and the 'running spiders' of the genus *Chiracanthium*. The woodlouse spider, easily recognised by its cream abdomen, red cephalothorax and legs, is quite common in urban areas. In Britain, this cosmopolitan spider, which often gets into houses, is responsible for most cases of spider bite. A bite on the leg, for example, may cause the limb to swell painfully for a period of two or three days, and dizziness can occur.

In Europe, latrodectism is confined to the Mediterranean region and is most prevalent in the Balkans (Dalmatia). There, the malmignatte has been described as causing a character-istically painful facial grimace, irrespective of where the site of the bite may be. The muscles of the jaw go into cramp and the face becomes sweat-covered with swollen eyes. Bites occur mostly during harvest time in periodic epidemics. Records at Pula Hospital, Istria, show that recent epidemics lasted from two to six years. In some years there seemed to be an infestation of spiders in the fields, but in others, the problem decreased and disappeared, sometimes for decades. When the spiders appeared again, farm workers may have forgotten about latrodectism. It is possible that the spider epidemics are related to the local abundance of grasshoppers or other insect prey.

An improbable, but true, report of spider bites at a sewage farm in Birmingham, England, in 1974, involved thousands of tiny 'money spiders' (*Leptohoptrum robustum*). It had never been imagined that such spiders, little more than one-tenth of an inch (2 mm) in length, could cause the slightest annoyance to man. But when maintaining the filter beds in the month of July, a number of workmen were bitten by swarms of these spiders, which dropped down their necks or crawled up their arms, causing inflammation and swelling. Subsequent investigation of the filter beds found astonishingly high numbers of the tiny arachnids living among the clinker – about 10,000 per cubic metre – vastly more than their normal density in a natural habitat.

The Uses of Spider Toxins

Many years ago, spider venoms were used by American Indians and the Bushmen of the Kalahari to paint their arrowheads. Today, researchers are investigating the potential of spider venoms in beneficial medicine. The partly digestive, necrotic venoms may, in particular, find a role in the dispersal of blood clots which cause heart attacks.

Spider toxins also have an important potential for use in safer kinds of insecticides. Previously it was thought that the size and complexity of neurotoxins such as latrotoxin would make them unsuitable as insecticides – because of cost and because the outer cuticle of insects would be a barrier to such large molecules. But, according to Dr Quicke, a researcher at Sheffield University, neurotoxins of small molecular size and high potency have been discovered and isolated from the spiders *Nephila* and *Argiope*. These toxins act on the insect neurotransmitter glutamate – their effect is to immobilise insects very quickly. However, Dr Quicke has expressed a doubt: what would happen if pest insects became resistant to insecticides derived from spider venom? Might they become resistant to spiders? Without effective predation by spiders, insects might become uncontrollable.

CHAPTER FIVE

EATING AND FIGHTING SPIDERS

WHY NOT EAT SPIDERS?

Compared with snails, caterpillars, juicy maggots and other insects, it must be admitted that spiders are not very popular foodstuffs. However, in South-East Asia, in Cambodia and Laos, it is a common sight to see by the roadside women selling satays of large, hairy, barbecued spiders (on a stick). And in parts of China, where they are also eaten, spiders are especially savoured because of their association with long life – due to the permanence of undisturbed cobwebs. Apparently, ten years is added to the life of a person who eats spiders. Thus, despite the aversion of Westerners to such creatures, it is a fact that a number of peoples around the world do relish them. These peoples include Indians in South America, the Bushmen of southern Africa, and the Aborigines or native Australians.

The spiders and insects which the Laotians love to eat were described by the English spider enthusiast, Dr W. S. Bristowe, who was not himself averse to tasting such delicacies. The Laotians will sample almost any reasonably sized spider but, in season, the giant orb-weaver (*Nephila*) is particularly sought after and eaten greedily. *Nephila* may be simply picked out of its web and the abdomen bitten off and eaten raw. Apparently its taste is mild and similar to that of raw potato mixed with lettuce.

But even more tasty is the favourite spider of the Laotians, the large, hairy, blue-legged tarantula (*Melopoeus*). This impressive spider lives under the ground in burrows. When Bristowe asked a local person the question, 'Are they highly valued?' he got an answer which could be translated literally: 'Find a hole and I will not leave it for another occasion.' Besides – however good these tarantulas may taste – they must also be a useful supplement to the diet because of their 60 per cent protein, 10 per cent fat, and rich mineral and vitamin content.

AN ACQUIRED TASTE

Brief notes for the culinary preparation of a blue-legged tarantula are as follows:

1 First dig out your tarantula.
2 Hold the head down with a stick and remove the fangs.
3 Place on a thin skewer and toast over a fire to remove hairs.
4 Serve the whole spider with salt or sliced with chillies.

Blue-legged tarantulas are said to taste when raw like hazel-nuts and when cooked like the marrow of chicken bones. With imagination many more dishes could be created – for example, *Tarantula Surprise* or *Arachnid à l'Escargot*. Bon appetit!

DON'T EAT THE HAIRS

Continuing Bristowe's fine tradition, the brave Rick West of Vancouver joined the Piaroa Indians of Venezuela in a meal of huge, 10-inch (25 cm) leg-span, 'goliath tarantulas' (*Theraphosa leblondi*). A dozen of the best were gathered by the young boys of the village who skilfully fished them out of their burrows with knotted vines, and wrapped them up in leaves. West described the first sighting of a spider: 'Beautiful and enormous, the leg span, thickness of legs and tennis-ball-sized abdomen is a sight not to be forgotten.' Back at the village, he managed to save some spiders from their fate but the rest were to be eaten. He described the cooking and eating (slightly abridged):

> The Piaroa know the urticarious effects of the abdominal hairs as I saw the men twist off the abdomens using a leaf. The contents and egg-roe are squeezed on to a broad leaf, rolled, folded and tied before being placed on the hot coals. The remaining carcass of the tarantula is placed in the fire for about two minutes. The specimen hisses and spits as the body juices seep out. Occasionally, the body is removed and patted between the hands like a tortilla to remove singed hair.
>
> When the body is removed to eat, the nearly ¾ of an inch (2 cm) fangs are detached and placed beside them. The abdominal contents are also removed which have 'hard-boiled' in the leaf. This material was very bitter. The carapace is peeled off to reveal a great deal of white cooked muscle. The entire spider, piece by piece, is eaten like shelling a cooked crab. The legs are eaten whole – I tried a couple and must confess, the taste was not bad – similar to prawns.
>
> When everyone was finished, the fangs were used as toothpicks to remove exoskeleton from between their teeth. I would have given anything for a cold beer to wash it all down.

A HUNDRED AT A TIME

An early reference to eating spiders for food comes from La Billardière on his voyage to New Caledonia:

> I observed by another fire two children who were regaling themselves with spiders of a new species, which I had very

frequently remarked in the woods, where they spin threads so strong that we were often exceedingly incommoded by them in our excursions. The children first killed them by shutting them up in a large earthen vessel which they were heating over a good fire; then they broiled them on the embers and ate them. They swallowed at least a hundred of them in our presence. We found in the sequel, on the same island, several other inhabitants who were searching eagerly for this sort of dish. So extraordinary, and at the same time so generally diffused a taste among these tribes, surprised us very much.

The inhabitants of New Caledonia call this species of spider *nouguee*, and I designate it by the name of *Aranea edulis* [currently = *Nephila edulis*].

Fighting Spiders

Spider fighting contests are very popular in a number of countries including South Africa, Malaysia, and the Philippines. The sport's popularity is perhaps greatest in the Philippines where it is known as *sabong ng gagamba*. Suitable contenders are collected during the season in the wetter months of June and July and also in December and January – the catching is done at night. There are a number of especially favoured and pugnacious species. The green *gagambang saging* ('banana spider') commands a premium price and the brown *gagambang bayabas* ('guava spider') is considered to be a 'trade secret' by some experts.

TRAINING A CHAMPION

In the Philippines, champion spiders are almost in a class with prize fighting cocks. Depending on the owner's inspiration, they are given names such as Adornado, Blue Diamond, 747, and Wonder Woman (of course, the females are the ones that fight). In training for a fight, meticulous preparation is the rule. Every day for a week before the event, they are soaked in water and then taken out to relieve themselves. With three days to go, the spider's regular diet is changed to dragonflies. By some strange chemistry, unknown to all except the experts, dragonflies make spiders strong and hungry.

THE BIG FIGHT

Glass-topped boxes constitute the arena for the gladiators, but some kinds fight their duel on a coconut leaf. Spiders are put on to the leaf's rib where they don't waste time chasing each other. Should they fall off, as they sometimes do, they are caught and placed back on. A spider that falls off twice is automatically declared the loser. Unlike other contests such as boxing or cock-fighting, where the opponents hit each other, the spider's weapon is sticky silk – the one that manages to envelop the other is the victor, while the vanquished gladiator simply becomes mummified.

It is said that spider-fighting is not a matter of skill or fierceness. Rather, it is a matter of size; the smaller combatant rarely prevails over a bigger adversary!

CHAPTER SIX

REMARKABLE SPIDERS

When Professor Comstock of Cornell University was asked by a visitor, 'What good are spiders?', he replied, 'What good are they? They are damned interesting!'

One can find spiders that catch their prey with a sticky globule on the end of a silk line. There are spider 'architects' that construct impressive webs and then take them down again in the morning. One can find caring, 'responsible' spiders that build nursery webs for their families while others carry the whole brood of spiderlings on their back. There are spider 'engineers' that tunnel into the ground and make secret passages for escape in case of intruders. There is even a unique spider 'frogman' that takes down an air supply to breathe under water. Many species preserve and store food for a 'rainy day' when no flies are about, but some crafty little types have turned to a life of crime and do nothing more than steal food from the webs of their bigger brethren. Still, there is actually one that knocks at the 'door' of another spider's home and waits for an answer before entering!

Spiders are found everywhere, and no place is too sacred for their occupation. The walls you lean against, the corners you look into, the books you begin to dust, the grassy lawns over whose soft beds you delight to walk, and even the flowers whose fragrances you enjoy, contain the spiders peculiar to each of these localities. Some there are that run, that spin, that dive, some that even dig to catch their prey –

thus pursuing several of the various crafts and industries of men – spinning, weaving, diving, and mining.

N. S. JAMBUNATHAN, India, 1905.

INTRODUCTION TO SPIDERS

Spiders are related to scorpions, mites, ticks and other arachnids. Almost 35,000 species of spiders in the world have been named so far, while possibly from two to five times that number remains to be discovered. Spiders are commonly thought of as one of the most successful groups of animals. They have existed for well over 300 million years and they live today in almost every kind of habitat. All are predators. Undoubtedly, their success is based on the many uses they have for silk. The largest species, South American tarantulas or 'bird-eating spiders', reach a body length of 4 inches (10 cm). The very largest, the goliath tarantula (*Theraphosa leblondi*) may have a leg span approaching the size of a dinner plate. But the tiniest species are really diminutive – about one twentieth of an inch (1 mm) in length.

DIFFERENT FAMILIES

Spiders are highly diversified and are classified in 105 families. The largest families include the: jumping spiders (family Salticidae, 4,400 species), money spiders (Linyphiidae, 3,700 species), orb-web weavers (Araneidae, 2,600 species), wolf spiders (Lycosidae, 2,200 species), tangle-web spiders (Theridiidae, 2,200 species), crab spiders (Thomisidae, 2,000 species), cob-web weavers (Agelenidae), funnel-web spiders (Dipluridae), trap-door spiders (Ctenizidae), huntsman spiders (Sparassidae), wandering spiders (Ctenidae), ogre-eyed spiders (Dinopidae), bolas spiders (Araneidae), spitting spiders (Scytodidae), raft spiders (Dolomedidae), recluse spiders (Loxoscelidae), and tarantulas (Theraphosidae).

SPIDER ANATOMY

A spider basically consists of two parts to the body joined by a narrow waist. The first half, the *cephalothorax* (combined head and thorax), contains the brain and carries the eight legs, the two leg-like *palps*, the jaws or pair of *chelicerae* (each with a movable fang to inject the venom), and the simple eyes – usually eight in number but variously arranged and developed according to the family. Most spiders have limited vision and rely mainly on touch.

The other half of the body, the *abdomen*, contains the heart, digestive tract, reproductive organs, respiratory openings and silk glands. The legs, of seven segments, have many tactile hairs to detect the slightest vibrations. Each leg ends in tiny claws and sometimes also a dense brush of hairs which gives adhesion on vertical surfaces. At the end of the abdomen are the spinning organs, the teat-like *spinnerets* (numbering two, four or six), from which strands of silk issue through tiny *spigots*. The adult male carries a pair of accessory sex organs on the ends of the two palps. The genital opening of both male and female is located on the underside of the abdomen.

LIFE CYCLE

Newly hatched spiders resemble tiny versions of the fully grown adults. In its growth from spiderling to adult, a spider undergoes approximately five to ten moults, each time sloughing the old skin, or *exoskeleton*, for a new, larger one. It is possible for lost or damaged limbs to be regenerated during a moult. Most spiders live for one or two years though female tarantulas and trap-door spiders can survive for up to twenty. At the other extreme, fast-living, tropical jumping spiders may live only a few months and pass through several generations in a year.

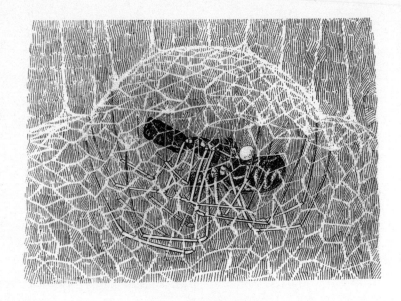

THE VARIOUS USES OF SILK

Besides the construction of webs, spiders have many other uses for silk. In fact, the 'web-less hunters', of which there are many kinds, build no webs at all yet employ silk in various other ways. Most spiders (hunters and web-builders) trail a *drag-line* and secure it behind them for safety – the spider climbing back up its drag-line is a familiar sight. Also, small spiders of many kinds use long airborne threads of silk to disperse (see Chapter 3). A very important use of silk is to construct nests and retreats, and to line burrows and attach trap-doors. Another essential use is in the making of egg sacs and cocoons. Many web weavers use silk to wrap up, or 'mummify', their prey, with a *swathing band*, while, in some species, the female may wrap up the male after mating. In the case of some crab spiders (*Xysticus*), the male ties the female with silk, the 'bridal veil', prior to mating. Before copulation, male spiders make a special *sperm web* (or line) on to which they deposit a couple of drops of sperm to be taken up in the 'syringe-like' palp organs.

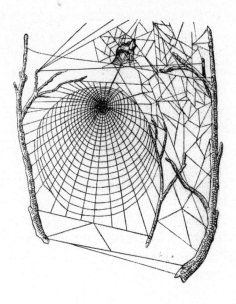

PREY CAPTURE

Spiders have devised many methods for catching their prey: trapping, ambushing, hunting and pirating. Their tactics are the result of a kind of 'arms race' over the last 300 million years. In general, spiders feed on live insects but many avoid ants, bugs and certain beetles – woodlice and millipedes are also unpopular. Lots of spiders are specialist feeders. Among the many such examples are the ladder-web spiders (*Scoloderus*) which are nocturnal moth catchers. In hot, dry places, black widow spiders (*Latrodectus*) may actually exist on a diet of scorpions caught in their tough webs. The mouse spider (*Scotophaeus*) will eat insects that are already dead; it will even eat museum insects on a pin. The golden silk or wood spiders (*Nephila*), with their large strong webs, intercept a wide traffic of flying insects and sometimes even small birds and bats. Spitting spiders (*Scytodes*) are highly unusual in that they catch their insect prey with gummy material ejected from the poison glands.

FEEDING

The body of the victim is punctured by the spider's fangs and paralysed or killed with the aid of venom. Before biting, some web spinners wrap the prey first in silk; others do it after biting. Digestive juices from the spider liquefy the inside of the prey so that it can be sucked out by the stomach's pumping action. An insect becomes just an empty shell, though spiders with strong jaws tend to mash their food to a pulp. In the case of tarantulas, trap-door, hunting and fishing spiders, the prey is not initially wrapped in silk, but simply seized, held by the fangs, and eaten. The spider's appetite may seem to be quite insatiable as the abdomen swells to absorb the food. However, when times are hard and prey is scarce, many spiders, especially the sedentary ones, can endure long periods, even months, without feeding. And many have no need to drink water directly.

In some situations there seems to be a distinct lack of suitable food. A letter sent to the author by a Mr Choate of Scotland described an inexplicable case of spiders imprisoned between panes of glass. He wrote:

My house has a small skylight in the roof. To cut out traffic noise I fitted a second pane of glass on the inside and sealed it with plaster. The two panes are about 9 inches (23 cm) apart and enclose a space of about 15 × 36 × 9 inches (38 × 90 × 23 cm). Some months after fitting I noticed a fair sized spider (about ½ inch (1.3 cm)) had spun a rudimentary web inside, in the bottom right hand corner, and I counted that it had been through 5 skin casts ranging in size from minute upwards. There were no signs of any insects or their remains between the two panes. The web (what there was of it) was littered with flakes of paint which had peeled off the sides of the skylight and there were numerous specks of what seemed to be excrement. I later removed the inner pane to clean it and then replaced it and sealed it up again. Now I notice that another spider has made a similar web in the same position though I can count only 3 skin casts. Again the web is littered with paint flakes and the glass is specked with excrement. No signs of insects or insect remains. The question is: how did these spiders manage to get in there and manage not only to survive but *grow*?

'Nobody feeds me. I have to get my own living. I live by my wits. I have to think things out, catch what I can, take what comes. And it just so happens that what comes is flies and insects and bugs. And further more,' said Charlotte, shaking one of her legs, 'do you realise that if I didn't catch bugs and eat them, bugs would increase and multiply and get so numerous that they'd destroy the earth, wipe out everything?'

E. B. WHITE, *Charlotte's Web*

EATING VERTEBRATES

The large tarantulas of South America (e.g. *Grammostola* and *Lasiodora*) are said to prefer sizeable quarry. The toxicologist Dr Vital Brazil of São Paulo kept many such tarantulas while experimenting on spider venoms, and fed them a diet of frogs, lizards and snakes. The tarantulas killed and ate foot-long (30 cm) pit-vipers and 18-inch (45 cm) rattlesnakes as readily as any other kind of small snake. Although large insects were also provided, the spiders ignored them in favour of the vertebrates. A colleague of Dr Vital Brazil wrote:

When a *Grammostola* and a young snake are put in a cage together, the spider tries to catch the snake by the head and will hold on in spite of all efforts of the snake to shake it off.

After a minute or two, the spider's poison begins to take effect, and the snake becomes quiet. Beginning at the head, the spider crushes the snake with its jaws and feeds upon its soft parts, sometimes taking 24 hours or more to suck the whole animal, leaving the remains in a shapeless mass.

Pliny's description, 2,000 years ago (see Chapter 9), of a spider killing a snake was not so fanciful after all!

In Australia, a barking spider (*Selenocosima*) is reputed to have dragged a chicken a considerable distance. A Mr Chisholm of Prairie Tableland, Queensland, wrote in 1919:

The tracks showed that it had been dragged. Following up we found the chicken 50 feet (16 m) away. When one of my people took hold of it there was tugging resistance. Investigation revealed the spider with one of the chicken's legs down the hole, which was about 1¾ inches (5 cm) in diameter.

Reginald Pocock of the British Museum, in his article on 'The Great Indian Spiders' described a large specimen of *Poecilotheria regalis* which was, when captured, devouring a small rat. There have also been many records (e.g. Robert Raven) of the much smaller black widow and redback spiders (*Latrodectus*) hoisting mice, lizards, and snakes into their webs. The large orb-weaver, *Nephila*, sometimes catches birds, as in the following account from Queensland by Miss J. A. Fletcher (1924):

One afternoon I saw a small bird apparently caught in nothing. From the distance its wings appeared to be folded at its sides, giving it an appearance of having stopped suddenly in the air. I ran to investigate, and found the bird, a Fly-eater (*Gerygone*) wrapped in a spider web. I cannot say how long it had been there, but it seemed too weak to struggle free . . . As I watched, a large black spider, with a greenish tinge, began to descend from a bunch of leaves . . . my sympathy for the bird came uppermost, and I seized a stick, smashed the web, freed the bird from the sticky stuff, when it flew away from my hands. The spider retreated to his den. Since then, I have wished my childish sympathy had waited to see what the spider would do.

COURTSHIP

Among the remarkable aspects of spiders, the mating habits rank highly and have attracted the attention of many biologists. Male and female spiders are often strikingly different in appearance. Adult males are recognised before any other features by their conspicuously enlarged palps. As a rule, females are larger than males of the same species but, sometimes, the male is so diminutive that he is able to avoid being taken for food and can climb without fear over the female's body.

Spider courtship is often a lengthy affair; besides partner recognition, the purpose is to replace the female's predatory instinct with a desire to mate. Courtship begins after the adult male has charged his palps with sperm. He abandons his normal habits and concentrates on finding a mate; web-spinning males become wanderers like the hunting spiders. Females are often detected by the scent left behind on their draglines. The male web spinner introduces himself by plucking the strands of the female's web. He is usually afraid of the female but eventually, after making the right vibrations, he approaches cautiously. Sometimes he waits for days and may make his move only when she is occupied with an insect or about to make her final moult. In the nursery-web spider (*Pisaura*), the male first gives the female a fly to unwrap. In spiders with good vision, such as wolf spiders and the brightly coloured jumping spiders, the males 'dance' before the females, waving their legs and palps and putting on special poses. In many species, an excited drumming of the palps occurs and some communicate through sound by rubbing parts of the body in the style of grasshoppers.

REPRODUCTION

In spiders the method of copulation is unique. Sperm from the male's genital opening is exuded on to the *sperm web* and taken up by the male's accessory sex organs – the palps. The sperm is transferred to the female by inserting the tip of a palp into the female's genital opening and squeezing the reservoir. The male and female organs fit together (in the same species) like a 'lock and key'. After mating, the male may need to be careful to avoid being eaten by the female. Sometimes 'battle-scarred' males with only three or four legs remaining can be seen having a last try. In any case, most males do not survive long after mating.

The female lays her eggs in one or more silken sacs, each containing from just a few eggs to a thousand or more in the larger species. Depending on the species, the cocoon may be suspended in a web or enclosed in a retreat, attached below a leaf, placed in a crevice or buried in the soil. Often they are cleverly camouflaged. Wolf spiders carry their egg sac around with them, usually attached to the spinnerets. In fact, they show a mother's attachment to their burdens, strenuously resisting attempts to take them away. Jean Henri Fabre, in *The Life of the Spider*, showed that a bereaved spider would accept false substitutes such as the cocoons of other spiders, cork balls, or pellets of cotton-wool. George and Elizabeth Peckham, of Milwaukee, discovered in 1887 that spiders possess a memory –

PLATE 1. Male and female 'Ladybird' spider (*Eresus niger*) recently rediscovered in the U.K. (*Paul Hillyard*)

PLATE 2. Mexican red-knee tarantula (*Brachypelma smithi*) on hand in the Insect House at London Zoo (*Paul Hillyard*)

PLATE 3 (*main picture*):
Spider in the bath (*Tegenaria parietina*) (*Paul Hillyard*)

Clockwise from top left:
PLATE 4. Banana spider
(*Heteropoda venatoria*)
(*Paul Hillyard*)
PLATE 5. Black Widow spider
(*Latrodectus mactans*)
(*Paul Hillyard*)
PLATE 6. Beautiful tarantula of
Sri Lanka (*Poecilotheria*)
(*Paul Hillyard*)
PLATE 7. Woodlouse spider
(*Dysdera crocata*) (*Paul Hillyard*)

PLATE 8. Underside of European garden spider (*Araneus diadematus*)
(*Paul Hillyard*)

PLATE 9. Kenyan jumping spider (*Goleba puella*) with eggs under leaf
(*Frances Murphy*)

an egg sac was re-accepted after 24 hours but not after 48 hours. The nursery-web spider, seemingly at great inconvenience to herself, carries the huge cocoon between her legs. Many others carry it in their jaws. Some egg sacs have an outer covering which is thin and meshy, some are quite tough and others, papery in texture; the shape may be flat or spherical. The young spiderlings emerge from the eggs after a few weeks or, very often, not until the following spring. They resemble miniature adults. In some species the parent takes care until they leave the nest but in others the young are on their own from birth. Often the spiderlings disperse on airborne lines of silk.

THE ENEMIES OF SPIDERS

Spiders are soft bodied and not distasteful; they thus have many enemies, for example birds, lizards, geckos, mammals, ants, centipedes, scorpions and other spiders. There are also myriads of insects and worms which parasitise the spiders or their eggs. Spiders seem to be most afraid of the spider-hunting wasps, among which the 'tarantula hawk wasps' are the largest wasps in the world. Many spiders seem to be defenceless when confronted with such a wasp – it stings the spider and uses it to provision its burrow. But the 'golden-wheeling spider' (*Carparachne*) of the Namib dunes, southern Africa, has a unique method of fleeing from the wasp: it throws itself side-ways and cartwheels down the dune. Another, the 'green lynx spider' (*Peucetia*) of Florida spits venom at its enemies. The spray can reach 8 inches (20 cm) and, according to Dr Linda Fink, it is stinging to the eyes.

A great many spiders rely on their mastery of the art of camouflage. Those coloured green live among leaves while red, yellow and white ones live among flowers; others are cryptic and blend well with backgrounds such as sand or lichen. Some crab spiders change colour according to the colour of the flower they are in. Some spiders are very difficult to see when motionless on a tree; some look like a twig, others resemble a bird's dropping. Some jumping spiders, and others, go about unrecognised because of their mimicry of ants – insects which many predators leave alone – the only obvious difference being their four pairs of legs instead of three in an ant. Some inhabit snail shells suspended clear of the ground by silk among vegetation. Such a shell, formerly occupied by a deceased mollusc, is a ready-made home. However, the labour necessary to haul a shell off the ground must be enormous considering that its weight is likely to be five or more times that of the spider.

Some Fascinating Spiders

TRAP-DOOR SPIDERS

Dr Willis Gertch of Arizona called the trap-door spiders the Houdinis of the spider world – 'one moment you see it, the next it is gone'. Trap-door spiders live underground in finely constructed tunnels which are excavated with their jaws. The burrows, from a few inches to more than a foot deep, are usually silk-lined and spacious enough to allow the spider to turn round. Many have a tight-fitting door which blends perfectly with the surface of the ground. Often all that can be seen is a hair-like crescent shape on the surface. When the spider feels the vibration of a passing insect, it lifts the door, rushes out, grabs the prey and returns to its burrow . . . to perform its disappearing trick.

Trap-door spiders are found throughout the hotter regions of the world. Their lifetime of several years is a solitary one but the burrow is a haven protected from heat and rain. They are classified in a number of families, of which the best known is Ctenizidae.

The American trap-door spider, *Bothriocyrtum californicum*, builds a thick, heavy door, made up of alternating layers of soil and silk, which fits in the opening like a cork in a bottle. When disturbed, the spider tenaciously holds the door down with its claws and fangs, bracing its legs against the side of the burrow. Even with the aid of a knife, a person has great difficulty in forcing it open. The strength of the spider was measured by Walker van Riper of Colorado Museum. He drilled two holes in the door, passed a loop of string through them and measured the pull with a spring scale. A force of fourteen ounces (0.4 kg) was indicated. As the spider weighs about one-tenth of an ounce (3 gm), the force is 140 times the spider's own weight. For a 150-pound (67 kg) man the equivalent would be over 10 tons. The

[87]

spider can keep this up for only a short time, so to make doubly sure, during the hottest part of the year when parasitic wasps are most active, the trap-door may be fastened shut and sealed with extra silk.

Many years ago, on the French Riviera around Menton, the same habits of construction and defence were observed among the local trap-door spiders by J. Traherne Moggridge who was a friend of Bates, Wallace, Pickard-Cambridge and Simon. Moggridge opened our eyes to the architectural skill of these spiders in his classic work, *Harvesting Ants and Trap-door Spiders* (1873). Its observations are original and its illustrations are delightful.

Moggridge distinguished two basic kinds of nest: the 'cork nest', with a thick door, and the 'wafer nest', with a thin, flexible door. He discovered that many nests are not just simple tunnels. Sometimes there is a second door – one which leads to a side-shaft. If an intruder enters, such as a centipede, the spider retreats to the branch tunnel and slams the door shut. In Australia, Dr Barbara Main has discovered that the trap-door spider, *Dekana*, builds in an escape route – a second hole on the surface loosely capped with sticks and stones through which it can easily push if threatened.

Moggridge was fascinated by the ingenuity of trap-door spiders. He lamented the fact that 'field naturalists' had made much less progress than 'cabinet naturalists' (in classification). The following is an extract from his book:

When at Hyères on the 11th of May, 1873, the evening being very warm and a bright moon shining, I went with my father and sister to see what the spiders would be doing on a hedge bank where we had previously marked five cork and eight wafer nests. The moonlight did not fall upon this spot, but I was provided with a lantern, and by its light the nests at first appeared to be tightly closed, but we soon perceived first one and then another with the door slightly raised, ready to close on the smallest alarm, whether from a footfall or from the flickering of the lamp. On either side of the raised door of one of the wafer nests I could see the feet of the spider projecting, and just at that moment I caught sight of a beetle close at hand, feeding on the topmost spray of some small plant below. I contrived to gather the spray without shaking off the beetle, and gradually pushed it nearer and nearer to the nest. When it almost touched the lip of the nest the door flew open, and the spider snatched at the beetle and dragged it down below.

For a few seconds the door remained tightly closed, and then, to our great surprise, was suddenly opened again, and the distasteful beetle was cast alive and unharmed out of the nest.

REMARKABLE JUMPERS

Jumping spiders (family Salticidae) are daytime hunters. When jumping, the take-off thrust comes from the last two pairs of legs while the first two reach out ahead for the landing. Jumps are mostly over short distances but can be up to twenty times the spider's length. The so-called Flying spider of Australia (*Saitis volans*) has wing-like extensions along the body which enable it to glide during leaps.

Jumping spiders have sufficient visual awareness to be able to turn and look at a person who looks at them. They can also see in colour – their pretty markings are displayed during courtship. Two of their eight eyes, the central front pair, are large and can recognise objects. Despite the small size of most jumping spiders, the central eyes are based on long tubes which work like miniature telephoto systems.

Having detected movement with the other eyes, a jumping spider turns to bring its central eyes to bear on the object. A jumper stalks its prey slowly, like a cat. The prey consists of insects such as flies, but also other spiders. When sufficiently close, the spider lowers its body, fastens a dragline to the surface, and then leaps on to the prey. But the spider does not necessarily approach in a straight-line. It may detour and temporarily lose sight of the quarry. In fact, detouring suggests a remarkable problem-solving ability for a spider. ('Why did the fly fly?' asked the old English riddle. Perhaps it was not realised how correct the answer was: 'Because the spider spied her.')

Jumping spiders also have the honour of holding the world altitude record. Major Hingston collected in the 1920s a number of specimens at 22,000 feet (7,000 m) on Mount Everest. Two species were named many years later by Fred Wanless as *Euophrys everestensis* and *Euophrys omnisuperstes*. According to Hingston:

> There was no sign of any other small creature at 22,000 feet; at this altitude all kinds of plant life had been left behind thousands of feet below. Finding the spiders by turning over stones was a great labour, partly on account of the exhaustion experienced at this altitude and partly because the stones were all frozen to the ground.

Since that initial discovery, it has been found that *Euophrys* feeds on tiny creatures which are part of a food chain based on plant material blown up from lower altitudes.

Most of the 4,400 species of jumping spiders live in the tropics; the family is highly diversified. One of the most extraordinary species is *Portia fimbriata* of tropical Australia. Because of its wide repertoire of hunting tactics it seems to be the cleverest of all spiders. *Portia* hunts in many different ways, including invading the webs of other spiders – which is most unusual. The typical hunting spiders usually move with great difficulty in webs; and web-building spiders are ill at ease in the webs of other kinds. But not *Portia* – it can move about and capture prey in all sorts of webs. It can even spin its own web, which is also irregular for a jumping spider. Sometimes *Portia*

The hard stare of Portia

builds its web adjacent to another spider so that when the neighbour follows an insect in hot pursuit, across *Portia*'s web, it can be attacked.

Portia is not pretty or colourful; in its cryptic posture it has a very curious, hunched appearance which looks nothing like a normal spider. In a web it is easily mistaken for a piece of rubbish; when walking it makes slow, jerky movements. But *Portia*'s jumps are quite impressive. The female measures about 1 cm and can jump, directly upwards, as much as 4–6 inches (10–15 cm). Upon landing, *Portia* either freezes or runs about 4 inches (10 cm) and then freezes. When invading the webs of other spiders, *Portia* makes vibrations to deceive the occupant. If it comes out, expecting an insect, *Portia* leaps on to it. When bitten, the victim usually runs some distance but becomes paralysed after 10 to 30 seconds. Sometimes, however, the host becomes alarmed and hastily 'decamps'.

When stalking normal jumping spiders, a particularly strange posture is adopted by *Portia*, one which is not used when pursuing a fly. Researchers Jackson and Hallas found that the jumping spider quarry did not recognise the slowly approaching

Portia as another salticid, or any sort of potential predator, or even as another animal.

Predation on other species of spiders is a dangerous occupation but *Portia* has a secret weapon – its exceptional vision. It can distinguish mates and prey at distances of up to 10 inches (27 cm); a 3 inch (7 cm) advantage over other jumpers. Not only is *Portia* the sharpest-eyed of all spiders, but, according to Professor M. F. Land its optical resolution is superior to all other terrestrial invertebrates, most of which have compound eyes. *Portia*'s principal eyes are of the 'simple' type and comparable with our own, but what is most remarkable is the tiny space they occupy – the size of the retinal receptors are close to the theoretical minimum, given the physical properties of light.

BOLAS SPIDERS

Bolas spiders hunt with sticky balls on the end of a line – they look like South American gauchos (cowboys) throwing their bolas. Usually the spider hangs from a simple horizontal thread and holds the bolas line with a leg – it swings or whirls the bolas at passing moths. When the ball sticks to a moth, the spider draws it up with the victim fluttering furiously. *Mastophora*, the American bolas spider (family Araneidae), and its relatives in Africa and Australia, are all plump-bodied, often strangely ornamented creatures which are rarely seen as they are active only at night. *Celaenia* in Australia does not even make a bolas – it simply hangs from a thread. Moths are captured when they fly straight into the spider's outstretched legs.

The explanation for these seemingly impossible methods of catching prey came in 1977. William Eberhard of the Smithsonian Institution discovered that all of the prey (in tropical America) were male 'armyworm' moths, even though many other kinds of moths were present.

Bolas spiders produce chemical compounds that imitate the moths' sex pheromone or scent – thus the male moths are lured directly to them. The pheromone is probably emitted from glands in the spider's forelegs. Moths always approach the spiders from downwind and are caught only at certain times of the night – the periods of sexual activity of the moths. Clearly, *Mastophora* is among the most specialised of all spiders. If no victim has come after an hour or so, the spider rolls the line into a ball of silk and eats it. Then she spins a fresh line, prepares another sticky bead or line of beads, and resumes her wait. During the day she clings to a twig and may resemble a bud or even a bird's dropping.

OGRE-EYED SPIDERS

The ogre-eyed, ogre-faced or net-casting spiders (*Dinopis*) have two enormous eyes and a remarkable method of catching prey. They live in tropical and subtropical regions. During the day *Dinopis* looks like a twig. After sunset it builds a highly unusual web, a silk net, and waits with it held between the long front legs. The spider hangs head-down on a thread, keeping a safe distance from ground predators. When an insect approaches, such as an ant, *Dinopis* opens the net, drops down, scoops it up, and springs back.

The spectacular appearance of *Dinopis* is due to its eyes. The front two are probably the largest simple eyes of any land invertebrate; they may be as much as one twentieth of an inch (1.4 mm) in diameter. The eye, taking into account its relatively short focal length, has an F-number of about 0.6 (greater than most camera lenses). Its light-gathering power is exceptional; it was described by Doctors Blest and Land as a 'fish-lens'. The retinal receptors are large and capable of absorbing 2,000 times more light per receptor than a jumping spider, most of which are active in the sunshine. In the darkness of the forest at night, a visual hunter like *Dinopis* needs all the light it can gather.

SOCIAL SPIDERS

Some spiders can be compared to social insects such as ants, termites and honey bees. Normally, spiders are known for their solitary and cannibalistic way of life. But some are gregarious and the extent of this ranges from loose aggregations, e.g. crowds of webs around a light, to the genuine, but few, cases of social life. All truly social spiders are web-building species and most live in the tropics where insects are abundant throughout the year. Communities can reach as many as 10,000 individuals. The advantages of togetherness are thought to include: safety in numbers, help in dealing with larger and stronger prey, and plenty of sexual partners, though fights among males often break out. Webs on the outside catch more insects but those inside get protection from predators and receive 'early warning' vibrations.

In contrast to insect societies, spider societies have no caste system or reproductive division of labour – all members appear to be fertile. Spider societies have *equality* in contrast to the systems of dominance in insects. Also, social spiders are noted for their tolerance to outsiders of the same species. Furthermore, an individual spider can probably survive outside the colony whereas an isolated insect cannot. Unlike insect societies, however, co-operative brood care is rare.

The Dome spider, *Cyrtophora* (*moluccensis* in South-East Asia and Australia, and *citricola* in Africa and the Mediterranean), is not highly social but hundreds of individuals may build immense assemblages of webs which resemble great 'spider cities'. The masses can reach far up electricity pylons or almost completely cover trees. The web is durable and each occupies up to 10 square feet (1 sq metre) with a complex of vertical lines and a domed, 'trampoline-like' sheet in the centre. The communities appear to be social but in fact individual spiders defend their webs and may attack intruding neighbours. However, death and injuries rarely occur. The young spiders are permitted to build their little webs within the framework of the mother's web.

A higher level of sociability is seen in the large orb-weaver, *Eriophora socialis*, of southern Brazil, Paraguay and Argentina. This is probably the very same species that was observed by Azara, Darwin and Masterman (see Chapter 8). As each author noted, a colony is comprised of one generation. Each spider defends its own orb-web and though there is no co-operation in prey capture, all roost together in a communal retreat. In a review of social spiders, Ruth Buskirk mentioned that *Eriophora* swops webs with other individuals and when roosting they all grasp each others' bodies – the 'large black mass' described by Masterman.

'El mosquero', *Mallos gregalis*, of Central Mexico is one of the most highly social of spiders. Mexicans bring sections of its web into the home as a protection against flies. The web is a complex sheet of woolly silk, covering bushes and other vegetation with a mass of silken galleries. Within the web are sheltered chambers; possibly the structure is designed to protect against sun and weather. Webs are constructed co-operatively and one spider may finish a task begun by another. When an insect becomes trapped in the web, several spiders approach, drag, pull and bite it, and then feed together. Many individuals, including adults of both sexes and immatures, may share the food.

In South Africa, social spiders are used in the battle against cockroaches and diseases spread by houseflies. The spider *Stegodyphus* is encouraged to build its untidy colonies in places like markets, restaurants, kitchens, abattoirs, dairies and latrines. They are said to work like a kind of fly paper, but are even better because there is no problem of insecticide-resistant flies. Also it is not easy to run short of spiders, and no care and attention is needed. Indeed, they can survive without food or water for at least six months. According to Dr J. J. Steyn (1959):

The nest is like a boarding-house, divided into many rooms in which each spider has its own little room or compartment. They all sit down together, as the whole community wages war against any insect that has fallen prey to their snares.

Unfortunately, however, the same kind of enthusiasm for it is not found in southern India. There, according to the forester Cedric Dover, it is considered to be a pest of mango trees. Whole trees can be covered and seriously debilitated with this spider's tough, woolly webbing.

SQUATTERS AND THIEVES

The kinds of spiders which side-step the need to build their own webs, and prefer instead to take advantage of others, are known as 'kleptoparasites' (from the Greek *kleptes*, a thief). In a large web it is difficult for the owner to patrol and keep out these kinds of tiny intruders and pilferers who move surreptitiously among the threads.

Small, silvery species of *Argyrodes* (family Theridiidae) are the best known kleptoparasitic spiders. They occur in the tropics and as far north as southern Spain. *Argyrodes* moves about in the host's web (e.g. *Nephila* or *Cyrtophora*), feeding on small neglected insects or sharing the host's prey. *Argyrodes elevatus*, for example, lives in the large golden orb of the Panamanian *Nephila clavipes*. The cheeky *Argyrodes* is adept at stealing sizeable prey which has already been wrapped up by the host. *Argyrodes* attaches lines to it and uses the 'derrick principle' to lift items many times their own weight. When 40 to 50 kleptos occur in a single web, the host may suffer considerable losses. Fritz Vollrath has observed that they also cut out sections of web and roll them up to eat. The silk is nutritious and likely to be garnished with adhering pollen grains and spores.

Often the large host, *Nephila*, becomes aware of the

activities of the *Argyrodes* and may attempt to chase them out of
the web. If the web becomes heavily infested, the host is likely
to leave the site and build a fresh web somewhere else. Thus the
kleptos do cause harm in a number of ways: by their steady
removal of food and by forcing the host to make a hazardous
departure. And kleptos may even attack the host when it is
vulnerable during its moults.

AQUATIC SPIDERS

The unique 'water spider', *Argyroneta aquatica*, lives under water
in lakes and ponds throughout Europe and Asia. A silken
'diving-bell' is constructed below the surface and stocked with
air taken down in bubbles which adhere to the hairy body.
Argyroneta looks silvery under water and because of its great
buoyancy it must swim down very energetically, with legs
flailing. When at rest in the air bell, it breathes normally, as if on
land.

Some normally terrestrial wolf spiders and money spiders
are also known to be capable of submerging for periods as long
as three weeks. Some breathe from a bubble of air which
surrounds the hairy body but others have no air bubble and they
absorb oxygen directly from the water, through the skin. The
remarkable 'semi-marine spider' (*Desis*) inhabits rock pools on
tropical and subtropical shores. This spider is able to survive for
days under the sea, without any bubble of air and no diving bell.
How it manages to do so is of great interest. Indeed, many
aspects of the life of *Desis* have still to be explained. How, for
example, does its body tolerate the salt without any obvious
adaptations?

The 'semi-aquatic', raft or fishing spiders (Family
Dolomedidae) are found worldwide. They live and hunt on the
surface tension of fresh water. Their legs, which radiate out, can
easily detect vibrations from insects; and they also catch small

fish. In Natal, South Africa, the Reverend Abrahams described their technique:

> I saw a little fish swim towards the stone and pass under the outstretched legs of the spider. The spider made a swift and sudden plunge. Its long legs, head, and body went entirely under water, the legs were thrown round the fish with wonderful rapidity, and in a moment the powerful fangs were piercing the body of the fish. The spider at once brought its catch to the rocks, and began without delay to eat it.

An interesting example of fishing was described by Carlos Berg in Argentina (1883). He wrote of the fishing spider (*Diapontia*) which builds a funnel-shaped net in shallow water:

> The object of its fishing is for tadpoles, those swift and slippery larval frogs. But the spider knows how to set up its apparatus and how to take its precautionary measures, in order that the toothsome morsel may not escape her. On the surface of the water, usually upon or between stones, where the tadpoles are wont to sun themselves, the spider constructs a two-winged or funnel-shaped net, a portion of which dips into the water. The tadpoles, without suspecting the cunning of the spider, venture into the net-like wing of the tissue or its funnel, and the spider skimming from behind upon the water drives on and finally overcomes one that has ventured deeper into the net. The shrivelled-up tadpole-skins surrounding the net convinced me of the skilfulness of the spider as a fisherman.

CHAPTER SEVEN

SILK AND WEBS

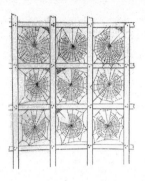

On foggy mornings, Charlotte's web was truly a thing of beauty. This morning each thin strand was decorated with dozens of tiny beads of water. The web glistened in the light and made a pattern of loveliness and mystery, like a delicate veil.

E. B. WHITE, *Charlotte's Web*

Perhaps the highest achievement of the spider's craft is the orb-web; its qualities of design and material are truly remarkable. Usually it is constructed at night – the spider relying on touch alone, without any visual feedback. It is quite ingenious how the line is initially laid across a gap, for example between two bushes, or over a small stream. In many hot countries, giant orb-webs, 6 feet wide (2 m) and more, festoon the telegraph wires and are suspended across forest paths. These great round webs are the work of golden-silk or giant wood spiders (*Nephila* species) which have bodies 2–3 inches long (7 cm) and legspans up to 8 inches (20 cm) across. Such webs are very tough and can ensnare small birds and bats. They will strongly resist any person walking through.

WEBS AS STRONG AS FISH NETS

As early as 1725, Sir Hans Sloane, in his book on Jamaica, wrote of a large wood spider which made nets 'so strong as to give a man inveigled in them trouble for sometime with their viscid, sticking quality. They will stop not only small birds but also wild pigeons.' In 1844, Jacobs, a traveller to Mauritius said: 'Their webs, nearly as large and strong as small fishing nets, and suspended in the open spaces, frequently and seriously retarded our progress.' In New Guinea, at the mouth of the River Fly, the Italian explorer L. M. d'Albertis (1880) observed many:

> A large kind of spider abounds to an extraordinary extent. It constructs a web from one branch to another at the height of a man from the ground, by which it causes the greatest inconvenience to those who walk in the island. In the middle of the web there is always a withered leaf, twisted round so as to form a small tube. The interior of this is covered with a very fine tissue, the work of the spider, who lurks therein. When an insect becomes entangled in the treacherous web, the hermit spider issues forth from his lair, seizes it, and takes it back with him to be eaten at his leisure.

Col. D. D. Cunningham, in his book *Plagues and Pleasures of Life in Bengal* (1907), said of spider webs at Calcutta:

> So strong, indeed, are they that even relatively powerful and vigorous birds may be taken captive by them – not that they ever remain hung up in the snares in their original position, but because, in tearing their way through, they carry away such masses of cordage closely wrapped around them as to render further flight impossible.

In *Two Years Among New Guinea Cannibals* (1906), the natural history collector, Mr E. A. Pratt, wrote this account of natives fishing with spider-web nets:

One of the greatest curiosities that I noted during my stay in New Guinea was the spiders' web fishing-net. In the forest at this point (near Yule Bay), huge spiders' webs, six feet in diameter, abounded. These were woven in a large mesh, varying from one inch square at the outside of the web to about one eighth inch at the centre. The web was most substantial, and had great resisting power, a fact of which the natives were not slow to avail themselves, for they pressed into the service of man this spider, which is about the size of a hazel-nut, with hairy, dark-brown legs spreading to about two inches. At the place where the webs are thickest they set up long bamboos, bent over in a loop at the end. In a very short time the spider weaves a web on this most convenient frame, and the Papuan has his fishing-net ready to his hand.

He goes down to the stream and uses it with great dexterity to catch fish of about one pound [0.45 kg] in weight, neither the water nor the fish sufficing to break the mesh. The usual practice is to stand on a rock in a backwater where there is an eddy. There they watch for a fish, and then dextrously flip it up and throw it on to the bank. Several men would set up bamboos so as to have nets ready all together, and would then arrange little fishing parties. It seemed to me that the substance of the web resisted water as readily as a duck's back.

An ingenious method of fishing was described by H. B. Guppy in his book *The Solomon Islands and Their Natives* (1887):

They first bent a pliant switch into an oval hoop, about a foot length, over which they spread a covering of stout spider-web. Having placed this hoop on the surface of the water, buoying it upon two light sticks, they shook it over a portion of a nest of ants, which formed a large kind of tumor on the trunk of a neighboring tree, thus covering the web with a number of struggling young insects. This snare was then allowed to float down the stream, when the little fish, which were between two and three inches long, commenced jumping up at the white bodies of the ants from underneath the hoop, apparently not seeing the intervening web on which they lay, as it appeared nearly transparent in the water. In a short time one of the small fish succeeded in getting its snout and gills entangled in the web, when a native at once waded in, and placed his hand under the entangled fish. With two of these web-hoops we caught nine or ten of these fish in a quarter of an hour.

E. W. Gudger was particularly interested in the accounts of spider-web fish-nets. He learnt from Captain C. A. Monkton (1918) that such nets were used by the natives of the Trobriand Islands, near New Guinea, to catch sluggish fish weighing up to three pounds (1.35 kg). The net was made by winding three or four strong webs across the fork of a branch. Gudger quoted a letter sent to him by Monkton:

> One peculiarity of the spider web was that in the water it appeared quite invisible to the human eye; the fork one could see but not the actual net. The net also did not appear to be very perishable, as I have seen natives take one from a wall where they have been resting for some days, make a patch or so, and go off fishing.

The accounts by Pratt and Guppy of fishing with spiders' webs were ridiculed by other writers including A. S. Meek in his book, *A Naturalist in Cannibal Land* (1913). However, Meek did observe that the New Guinea natives captured enormous birdwing butterflies 'with nets made most ingeniously with spiders' webs'. Indeed, in view of the weight of evidence the doubters were probably mistaken. From the testimony of so many writers it seems that the fishing nets are, or were, quite genuine. All the above accounts probably refer to the 'golden silk spiders', or 'giant wood spiders', of the genus *Nephila*.

Native of New Guinea with spider web fishing net

Building the Orb-Web

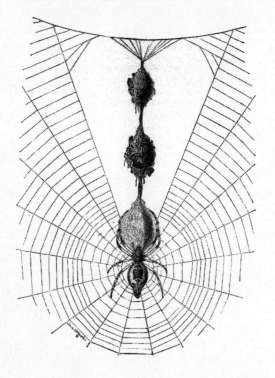

'What's miraculous about a spider's web?' said Mrs Arable.
'Ever try to spin one?' asked Mr Dorian.

E. B. WHITE, *Charlotte's Web*

Considering all its complicated connections, angles and
tensions, the two-dimensional orb-web is an amazing feat of
engineering. It is a type of web constructed by about 3,000
species of spiders, mostly in the family Araneidae. Often it is
possible to identify the species of spider from particular details of
the web's construction. Observing the whole building process
needs luck and patience, especially in the early stages which are
often interrupted by long pauses.

'When are you going to spin a web?' asked Wilbur.
'This afternoon, late, if I'm not too tired,' said Charlotte.

E. B. WHITE, *Charlotte's Web*

To start construction, the spider moves from her hiding place to take up a prominent position. Using the breeze, a silk line of the very finest filaments is wafted out, but in calm conditions, the line may be initiated by dropping down on a dragline. After climbing back up, the resulting loop of line is floated on to the air. The spider waits, as if fishing, until this first line, the 'spanning thread', touches and adheres to an object across the gap. Feeling the thread fixed, she tightens it and runs across, back and forth, creating a stout cable of many strands: the 'bridge thread'. Then, from the middle of the bridge thread, the spider attaches a line, drops down and fixes it below. Under tension, the resulting 'Y'-structure marks the centre ('hub') and first three 'radii' of the future orb-web.

After fixing some 'mooring threads' (guy-lines), the next stage establishes the many radii (from 10 to 80 depending on the species) which radiate from the hub to near the edge of the orb, outlined by the 'frame threads'. At the hub, the spider decides on the sector in which the next radius is to be placed. Each radius is produced twice, the first temporarily on the outward movement; then cut and replaced by the permanent line laid on return to the hub. Normally, the angles between the radii, measured by the spider's legs, are very consistent – in the case of the garden spider (*Araneus diadematus*), the 24 to 30 radii are placed about 12–15 degrees apart.

While the spider is busy placing the radii, a complex of threads develops at the hub, where she may sit when the web is complete. The hub is reinforced and surrounded by three or four circular threads: the 'strengthening zone'. From this zone, the 'temporary spiral' is laid out towards the edge of the orb – it ties the radii together and serves as a non-sticky guide-line when the permanent 'sticky spiral' is put down on return to the hub (simultaneously cutting out the temporary spiral). As one of the spider's front legs reaches for the next radius, a fourth leg pulls the sticky thread from the spinnerets, dabs it against the radius, and gives a tug so that it breaks up into sticky beads. But the spiral thread does not simply go round and round; a number of 'turning points' can be seen where the spider has reversed direction by 180 degrees. Before reaching the hub, the spiral thread terminates, leaving a space between it and the hub, the 'free zone' – where the spider can dodge from one side of the web to the other. In some species, the hub is removed to perform the same function as the free zone.

The entire web may be completed in approximately one hour, the sticky spiral being the longest operation. Experiments have found that spiders do not just automatically follow the procedure, without being aware of how it is shaping-up; they continually adjust the loadings and tensions. Major Hingston in 1920 found that if a radius is removed it is immediately replaced by the spider. Hingston wrote: '. . . testing the radii is of great importance, for the absence of a radius means a loss of symmetry. Thus the spider is most diligent in this stage of its duty.' Professor P. J. Peters, in 1970, experimented by transferring spiders which had just built their spiral threads, to other webs without spiral threads. Usually when the spider found that the spiral was lacking, it promptly repeated the job.

> The spider's touch, how exquisitely fine!
> Feels at every thread, and lives along the line
> ALEXANDER POPE

The combined length of the threads in a web is about 60–200 feet (20–60 m) for a garden spider. Hingston calculated: 'With the exception of the foundation lines . . . the spider emitted 122 feet of filament, made 699 attachments and travelled over a distance of 178 feet. Yet the whole was woven into a circular web 22 inches in diameter and occupied the spider only 36 minutes.'

And how many webs are constructed in a spider's lifetime?
Perhaps 100. At less then one milligram, webs are extremely
light; rolled into a ball, one is likely to have the size of a rice
grain.

When the web with all its mooring threads and final touches
are finally completed, the spider settles on the hub, or retires to a
retreat where it is in touch with the web through a 'signal thread'
held by a front leg. Females are usually much more conspicuous
in webs than males.

> Day after day the spider waited, head–down, for an idea to
> come. Hour by hour she sat motionless, deep in thought.
>   E. B. WHITE, *Charlotte's Web*

HOW WEBS CAPTURE PREY

Spiders' webs are designed primarily to catch insects. The
Reverend Henry McCook (see Chapter 10) counted as many as
250 insects caught in a single web. The ability of orb-webs to
stop and retain plenty of insects is influenced by a number of
factors including: their location and height above ground (more
insects lower down), the ability to absorb momentum, the
quality of the adhesive, and the density of silk threads.

Orb-webs need to be capable of preventing the escape of
flying or jumping insects for at least 5–10 seconds until the spider
arrives to attack. From the moment of impact, a garden spider
(*Araneus diadematus*) takes about 5 seconds to bite and begin
wrapping up a housefly. Those webs with the advantage of
restraining prey for longer periods have been favoured by
natural selection – spiders need extra time to approach large and
vigorous insects. Different species of spiders vary in their attack
behaviour. Some bite first and then wrap the victim in silk;
others wrap first, which is useful when dealing with stinging
insects such as ants. Very aggressive insects, and those that

discharge noxious chemicals, are likely to be carefully cut out of the web by the spider.

Webs need to be able to resist the impacts of prey, detritus, wind and rain. Besides the strength of the material, the design, geometry, and distribution of tension among the threads are all critical factors. Webs with a higher density of radii can absorb greater energy and are able to catch heavier and faster-moving insects. They also collect greater numbers of smaller insects. On the other hand, however, a dense web is more visible during the day and more extravagant in the use of silk – the protein used in silk is an expensive resource.

In building the web the spider takes account of the developing loads and tensions and tries to equalise the tensions so that the stress in all members is the same – better to resist the stress of sudden impacts. In an orb-web, there are usually more radii in the lower half of a web – the spider thus takes account of the fact that these will be under less tension than those in the upper half. Also, if the spider sits at the hub, the upper radii will be under increased load. Probably the reason why spiders cut out each radius during construction, only to replace it on return to the hub, is to ensure that the permanent radius is laid with the correct tension.

FABRE'S OBSERVATIONS

There are no masters nor apprentices in their guild; all know their craft from the moment that the first thread is laid.

J. H. FABRE, *The Life of the Spider*

Fabre, the 'insect man' of France, wrote affectionately, in the 1870s, of a favourite spider in his garden at Serignan in Provence:

This one is a matron; she dates back to last year; her majestic corpulence, so exceptional at this season [July], proclaims the fact. I know her as the Angular Epeira [*Araneus angulatus*].

She has taken up her abode, at a convenient height for observation, between a row of cypress-trees and a clump of laurels, near the entrance to an alley haunted by moths. The spot appears well-chosen, for the Epeira does not change it throughout the season, though she renews her net almost every night.

Punctually as darkness falls, our whole family goes and calls upon her. We stand amazed at her wealth of belly and her exuberant somersaults in the maze of quivering ropes; we admire the faultless geometry of the net as it gradually takes shape. All agleam in the lantern-light, the work becomes a fairy orb, which seems woven of moonbeams.

What delightful, simple evenings we have spent looking into the spider's workshop!

Jean Henri Fabre wondered about the ability of orb–weavers to repair damaged webs. While he watched a spider building a new web, a great insect blundered into it. The spider dealt with the insect but then resumed building the spiral thread and simply ignored the torn part. Fabre wrote:

This is no case of distraction, of individual carelessness; all the large spinstresses suffer from a similar incapacity for patching. The Angular Epeira re-makes her web nearly every evening; the Banded Epeira [*Argiope bruennichi*] and the Silky Epeira [*Argiope lobata*] reconstruct theirs only very seldom and use them even when extremely dilapidated. They go on hunting with shapeless rags. Never any repairs; never; never. I am sorry, because of the reputation which our hard-pressed theorists have given her, but the spider is absolutely unable to mend her work.

Fabre's observations, made over one hundred years ago, can be compared with those of McCook (see Chapter 10), who said that spiders do make repairs, and the more recent experiments of Hingston and Peters, above. The question of why spiders don't stick to their own webs was explained by both Fabre and Hingston: as far as possible, spiders walk on the non-sticky radii but, in addition, the legs are groomed with an oily coating which does not stick. However, a spider may get stuck if it happens to be in the web of another kind. And it is said that an orb-spider picked up and thrown back into its own web will also stick!

To appoint one's self an inspector of spiders' webs, for many years and for long seasons, means joining a not overcrowded profession . . .

J. H. FABRE, *The Life of the Spider*

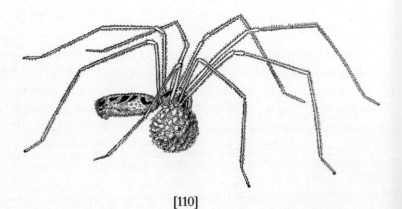

THE PRODUCTION OF SILK

What a number of products to come from that curious
factory, a spider's belly! I behold the results, but fail to
understand the working of the machine. I leave the problem
to the masters of the microtome and the scalpel.

J. H. FABRE, *The Life of the Spider*

Inside the abdomen of a spider are from one to six different
kinds of spinning glands (the greatest number in the orb-
weavers). Each type of gland secretes a particular kind of silk
and leads to a particular spinneret. One gland for example
produces the sticky silk of the catching spiral, another the
dragline silk, and another the swathing silk. In the spinning
glands, syrup-like blends of liquid protein are manufactured in
soluble form but, when pulled from the spigots, or little nozzles,
of each spinneret, the fibres become solid and insoluble. The
conversion is due to a change in the orientation of the molecules;
at the same time, the molecular weight of the soluble protein
changes from about 30,000 to 200,000 – 300,000 in the solidified
silk.

Spider silk is very strong but extremely fine. A typical
strand of garden spider silk has a diameter of about .00012 inch
(.003 mm), approximately one tenth the diameter of silkworm
cocoon silk. For an equal diameter, spider silk is stronger than
steel and about as strong as nylon. It is, however, much more
resilient and can stretch several times before breaking – it is
twice as elastic as nylon and more difficult to break than rubber.
The energy required to break spider silk (its 'toughness') is about
ten times that of other natural materials such as cellulose,
collagen and chitin. Dragline silk (about .00032 inch (.008 mm)
in *Nephila*) is especially strong – approximately twice that of silk
from the silkworm. Spider silks are proteins; their structure is a
composite of crystalline (30 per cent) and non-crystalline regions

(70 per cent). The different regions can change structure under tension and move in relation to each other. The silk is affected by rain and absorbs water, causing it to swell and shorten (unlike nylon and silkworm silk). It returns to normal after drying. Spider silk is very durable and is insoluble in organic solvents. Very harsh acids are needed to break it down in order to study the protein units. And old abandoned cobwebs are not attacked by fungi and bacteria – probably because of their acidity.

The kind of silk combed out by 'cribellate' spiders, from a special organ additional to the other spinnerets, is particularly fine and woolly. It lacks the beading of gluey silk, but still has a 'sticky' effect and a great ability to snag the legs of insects. It weathers well and does not need frequent renewal like webs made with gluey silk – they lose their stickiness quickly. Orb-webs made with cribellate silk, for example by spiders in the family Uloboridae, are usually more or less horizontal but otherwise similar in design to those made with gluey silk, mostly by the family Araneidae. Cribellate silk is the 'original Velcro' according to Jacqueline Palmer of Harvard, an expert on silk.

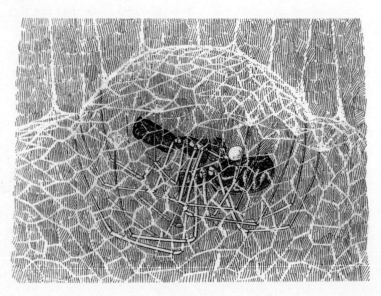

Different Kinds of Webs

A great diversity of spiders' webs exists on the planet; many still await description. Some are designed to catch flying insects, others jumping insects and yet others crawling insects. A few specialise in catching moths – these are built at night and then removed at dawn. Other webs, such as those of *Argiope*, are targeted at grasshoppers during the daytime. A great many, such as those of *Nephila*, operate both day and night. Some webs are extensive, some are built gregariously, while others are no more than a solitary thread. Some webs are sticky to the touch, others dry, and others woolly. Many orb-weavers renew their webs daily, whereas most sheet-weavers continue to add to the sheet long after it is built. And some webs, such as the 'nursery web' of the European *Pisaura*, have a secondary purpose, such as protection of the young.

PRIMITIVE WEBS

The kinds of webs considered to be most primitive are the simple tube-webs which radiate 'fishing lines' from a hole, e.g. in the European *Segestria*, or perhaps from a silk-lined burrow. Such a web does not actually capture prey but only transmits vibrations from a passing insect; the spider rushes out from its retreat and grabs it. This type is seen also in *Liphistius* of South-East Asia, though in this case the lines radiate from a silken trap-door. One of the strangest kinds of webs is the silken-tube of the 'purse-web' spider *Atypus* (Northern Hemisphere). Like a gloved finger, the web emerges from the soil as the extension of a silk-lined burrow. When a fly alights on the tube it is attacked through the fabric by a massive pair of fangs belonging to the spider which lives inside. The victim is dragged in and later the break is mended. Normally, only the male *Atypus* leaves its burrow – when searching for a mate.

SHEETS AND THREE-DIMENSIONAL WEBS

Of all webs, some of the most ubiquitous kinds are the more or less horizontal sheet-webs and cobwebs. Some have a tubular retreat at one end and may be called funnel-webs. Some spiders walk on top of their sheet (as in the European *Agelena*), while others hang upside down below (as in the cosmopolitan *Linyphia*). Often these horizontal webs become three-dimensional with criss-crossing vertical threads, or 'scaffolding', to intercept flying insects and knock them on to the sheet. *Linyphia* shakes its web to assist the insect's descent, and then bites through the web to pull the victim through. Damage to the web is mended later.

Other three-dimensional webs include: tangle-webs, frame-webs and mesh-webs. Tangle-webs, such as those of the black widow spider, *Latrodectus*, are somewhat irregular but three structural levels can be recognised: an uppermost complex of supporting threads; a central zone of tangle threads; and a lower zone of vertical trap threads. The trap threads, under tension, are beaded with gluey droplets near their attachment to the ground. Insects crawling over the ground may break the attachment and, getting stuck to the line, find themselves lifted off the ground towards the spider waiting among the tangle-web. The impressive 'dome web' of the subtropical *Cyrtophora*, has a sheet of fine netting, resembling a horizontal orb-web, surrounded above and below with an irregular mesh of threads functioning as a 'Knock-down maze'.

UNUSUAL KINDS OF ORB-WEBS

Besides the familiar kinds of orb-web, there are some unusual forms which range from the impressive 'ladder web' of the tropical *Scoloderus*, to the rudimentary 'asterisk web' of the

Eastern USA *Wixia ectypa*. The ladder web takes three hours to build and may be up to 3 feet (1 m) tall – in New Guinea it is spun with an orb at the top of the ladder, while in Colombia the orb is at the bottom. These webs are more effective against moths than regular orb-webs. After collision with a ladder web, moths, which are normally 'non-stick' because of their loose scales, tumble down and may get stuck near the bottom, having lost many scales. Like *Scoloderus*, *Wixia* also spins at night but, according to Mark Stowe, takes only two minutes to construct its web which resembles an unfinished orb. The asterisk web has a simple hub and eight radii which are usually positioned between a fork in the branches. The spider moves to attack passing insects.

Some orb-webs are noted for the position in which they are built. The attractive *Herennia ornatissima* of South-East Asia builds its orb-web remarkably close to a tree trunk or rock. In this position the web is virtually invisible – insects such as dragonflies may alight on the tree trunk without suspecting anything. And many smaller orb-weavers, like *Araniella* of Europe, manage to build their web within the curl of a leaf. There is even one spider (the South American *Wendilgarda*) which lowers its web on to the surface of streams to trawl for aquatic insects.

Orb-webs constructed by the family Uloboridae often resemble the regular webs of the Araneidae, though their silk differs. The 'triangle-web' spider (*Hyptiotes*) of the Northern Hemisphere is an unusual member of the family Uloboridae. The web consists of three sections of an orb forming a triangle. The signal thread is held by the spider's front legs while the mooring thread goes from the spider's spinnerets to the vegetation. When prey arrives, *Hyptiotes* releases the spring-like tension with extra silk thread and the web collapses around the prey. An even more unusual form of web is the 'orb-plus-cone web' of a South-East Asian *Uloborus*. Its complex construction involves building two orb webs. The first is pulled out into a cone and the second built within the open circle of the cone. It takes about three hours to complete. The whole thing forms a kind of 'cage' around the spider and presents surfaces on all sides to trap prey. Other cribellate weavers are also highly specialised and include *Dinopis*, the 'net-casting spider' (see Chapter 6) which, holding its web between its legs, uses it as an offensive weapon.

DECORATED WEBS

Some webs, especially those constructed by *Argiope, Cyclosa* and *Uloborus*, are distinguished by their decorative bands, zigzags and spirals known as *stabilimenta*. The purpose of these

PLATE 10. Giant orb-weaver female (*Nephila senegalensis*) in savannah
(*K. G. Preston-Mafham/Premaphotos Wildlife*)

PLATE 11 (*main picture*):
Webs in the mist (*Paul Hillyard*)

Anticlockwise from far left:
PLATE 12. European Fishing spider
(*Dolomedes*) (*Paul Hillyard*)
PLATE 13. Ant-mimicking spider in Nepal
(*Myrmarachne*) (*K. G. Preston-Mafham/
Premaphotos Wildlife*)
PLATE 14. Crab spider (*Synema*) and insect
among flower in Spain
(*Paul Hillyard*)

PLATE 15. Triangle spider (*Hyptiotes paradoxus*) holding its web
by the signal thread (*Paul Hillyard*)

PLATE 16. *Herennia ornatissima* female on orb-web in Malaysia
(*Paul Hillyard*)

embellishments is probably not for stabilisation, but rather for camouflage, though to the human eye they seem highly conspicuous. They look like a kind of spider's 'signature', especially because of the great variability among individuals. Various explanations and purposes for the stabilimenta have been suggested; possibly they serve several different functions. Perhaps they are for camouflage or predator distraction; maybe they are warnings to large insects or birds not to blunder into a web; or maybe they are devices to adjust the tensions among the silk lines. In some cases a stabilimentum might be connected with the spider's pumping movements when shaking the web. The effect of the stabilimentum could thus be to increase the apparent size of the spider and deter predators. The latest explanation is that the zigzags reflect ultra-violet light, as flowers do, and so may be attractive to insects.

REDUCED WEBS

Some webs are reduced to a single thread, or possibly just two or three in an 'H' shape. These minimal webs are derived from ancestors with 'normal' orb-webs or scaffolding webs. They vary in their details of operation: the sticky globules may be placed where the thread attaches to a branch (as in the European *Episinus*); or in the centre of the line between attachment points (as in the American *Phoroncidia*); or at the far end of a line attached to a spider's leg (as in the American *Mastophora*); or there may be no sticky globules at all, as in the worldwide *Miagrammopes*. One might expect these reduced webs to be much less effective than typical multiple-thread webs. However, they do catch many more insects *per thread* than normal webs. They are inconspicuous and single threads are actually attractive to some insects to alight on. Many reduced-web spiders are specialist feeders and their tactics can include additional attacking behaviour and sometimes 'attractant' chemicals. The ultimate reduction of webs is seen in the Australian *Archemorus* which builds no web at all but just sits on a silk pad, on a leaf, and seizes prey with its heavily spined front legs. It has come to resemble the crab spiders.

Some spiders, known as kleptoparasites, have given up making their own webs (e.g. *Argyrodes*) and have turned instead to invading the webs of others (see Chapter 6). Some, like the pirate spiders (e.g. *Mimetus*), are specialists which prey on web-building spiders.

THE EARLIEST WEBS

Because of their extreme fragility, spiders' webs have not survived as fossils. We can thus only theorise about how the orb-web evolved from more primitive kinds. Probably, millions of years ago, the original spiders' webs were little more than extensions of silk from a hiding place. As spiders darted out they trailed their draglines behind them. The lines at first acted as simple trip-lines to signal the approach of prey. Later the webs diversified; they extended outwards, some developed into horizontal sheets, some became 'trampoline-like' structures; and finally, some webs turned upright and became two-dimensional nets with the spider sitting at the centre. It is possible that the evolution from sheets to nets was a response to the appearance of flying insects in addition to the original crawling kinds.

While there are no fossil webs, there are fossil spiders and the earliest evidence for the production of silk comes from a fossil spinneret found in Middle Devonian rocks (about 380 million years old) near Gilboa, New York. It is claimed to be the oldest spider fossil and is believed to pre-date the evolution of flying insects – the prey for which aerial webs are designed. The spinneret is a single segment carrying 20 spigots (nozzles); it resembles that of the 'living fossil' (*Liphistius*), the giant trap-door spider of South-East Asia. This primitive spider uses silk to line the burrow and to make a door with trip-lines extending out.

The extinct *Megarachne*, a giant fossil mygalomorph from the Carboniferous of Argentina (about 300 million years ago), is thought (P. A. Selden) to have been the largest spider of all time. The length of this formidable beast was about 13 inches (33 cm) while its legspan was probably about 20 inches (50 cm). *Megarachne* had large chelicerae and a flat rigid plate on the abdomen.

BUILDING WEBS IN OUTER SPACE

NASA constructed a laboratory, called Skylab, in which experiments could be conducted in zero gravity, outside the Earth's atmosphere. Sending spiders up in Skylab, to see how they performed in weightlessness, was a prize-winning proposal by a high school student from Lexington, Massachusetts, though the original idea came from Dr Peter Witt of North Carolina. When the Apollo spacecraft with Skylab II and three astronauts was launched on 28 July 1973, two spiders (*Araneus diadematus*), together with two flies, were taken up. A week after lift off, spider number one was placed on a frame in a cage; spider number two was kept in a small tube until being released on to the frame four weeks after launch.

According to Dr Witt:

Seeing the spiders in space [on TV] was for me very exciting and worth all the years of waiting. I saw something which no human eye had ever observed before. Spider number two floated slowly when introduced into the cage; it touched the frame, bounced back and floated in the opposite direction. Its legs were extended and hardly moved. The silk, which one could observe coming from the spinnerets at the end of the abdomen, wafted in wide waves through the air. On

[119]

earth it would have been stretched tight by the spider's weight. The spider obviously missed its usual clues. It could no longer handle the situation in an appropriate way and presumably waited for what would happen next.

The other spider, number one, after three weeks' trial and error, had adjusted to the conditions sufficiently well that it 'ran very competently along its strand of silk to escape from the astronauts'.

The experiment undoubtedly succeeded in showing that spiders can build orb-webs in zero gravity. The two spiders needed to adjust to the very strange conditions but their work differed only in minor details from Earth webs. Curiously, in outer space the webs were perfectly symmetric, while on Earth they are usually asymmetric: the lower half is larger, with more radii, than the upper. Also, the spiral simply went round and round without any interruption – there was a low number of turning points. These differences in construction were attributed to the absence of gravity as a cue.

> I'm told that the spider
> Has coiled up inside her
> Enough silky material
> To spin an aerial
> One-way track
> To the moon and back
> Whilst I
> Cannot even catch a fly
> ANONYMOUS

The Uses of Spiders' Silk

NOVELTY USES

During the eighteenth and nineteenth centuries there were a number of vain attempts to commercialise spider silk. The results unfortunately produced nothing more than curiosities. Xavier Saint-Hilaire Bon of Montpellier presented to the French Academy, in 1709, several pairs of silk gloves and stockings made from spiders' cocoons. In the same year, he described his work in a *Dissertation on the usefulness of spider's silk*. To find out if the products were genuine, the Academy invited the physicist René Réaumur to investigate. His resulting paper, *Examen de la soye des araignées* (1710) pointed out the inherent difficulties. First, the cannibalistic nature of spiders meant that they must be kept apart. Second, because spiders' silk is so fine, only egg-cocoon silk was strong enough; also unfortunately it lacked the lustre of silkworm silk. Réaumur calculated that in order to produce a pound of silk, 27,648 female spiders (*Araneus diadematus*) would be required. Furthermore, a vast quantity of flies would be needed for food. He concluded that spiders' silk was unlikely to become a serious rival to that of the silkworm. However, Bon's and Réaumur's papers aroused the curiosity of the Emperor of China who requested translations. In a strange story dating from 1858, in the magazine *Atlantic Monthly* the Emperor Aurengzebe of Hindustan is reported to have scolded his daughter for the indelicacy of her costume, even though she was wearing seven thicknesses of spider silk. In 1876, a Chinese delegation visited Europe and the ambassador presented to Queen Victoria an elegant silken gown which had been made entirely from thousands of spiders' webs.

Early in the nineteenth century, the Burgmann family of Innsbruck earned their living by painting on spider silk. One of their paintings, the 'Madonna and Child' is preserved between sheets of glass at Chester Cathedral, England, and another is at the Smithsonian Institution, Washington. The fine material is transparent and equally effective from either side. Even today, a few people still make parchments, suitable for painting, from many layers of cobwebs and a little milk. For the simple pleasure of their delicate beauty, the American, C. L. Stong, collected webs by spraying them with lacquer and mounting them on a sheet of paper . . . 'Even people who abhor spiders acknowledge that spider webs are compositions of remarkable beauty when they are transferred to backgrounds of colour and placed in appropriate frames on walls.'

Professor B. G. Wilder of Charleston, South Carolina, developed a silk reeling machine in 1865. This ingenious device resembled a set of 'stocks' to hold spiders and draw out their silk on reels. Using the species *Nephila plumipes* which produces lustrous silk in greater quantity and strength than *Araneus diadematus*, the professor proved that *Nephila* can control, at will, the thickness and colour of the thread, either yellow or white. He wound off silk at the rate of six feet per minute with a total output of 450 feet (140 m) per hour. When the professor opened up a spider's abdomen after two hour's reeling, he found the glands were still partly filled with liquid silk. Wilder was optimistic about spiders' silk but in the end was defeated by the practical difficulties of commercial production.

The Rev P. Camboué, in 1892 tried to collect and utilise the beautiful, strong yellow silk of the huge *Halabe* spider of Madagascar (*Nephila madagascariensis*). It was hoped to make lightweight ropes, but, again, the venture was unsuccessful. However, the natives of the New Hebrides do in fact use the web of a similar spider as a kind of cloth to make small bags in which they keep arrow-heads and tobacco (Gaggin, 1900). During the Second World War, fine silk threads from black widow spiders in America, and from garden spiders in Britain, were used for the cross hairs of telescopic gun sights. Still finer threads can be obtained from gossamer spiders on sunny autumn mornings.

BIRDS' NESTS

Spiders' silk is an ideal medium for binding together nest material. The hermit-hummingbird uses silk to suspend its nest from a leaf and the African tailor bird uses it to stitch leaves together. Long-tailed tits in Europe make their nests with a combination of spiders' webs and lichen. In Australia, N. L. Roberts recorded more than a hundred species of birds which use spiders' webs or cocoons for building, or decorating, nests. The willie-wagtail has a cup-shaped nest which uses so much silk that it has a matted, greyish appearance; the rock warbler's nest may be suspended from the roof of a cave – it was described thus:

> The supporting flat mass of silky spiders' webs is composed for about two inches, sometimes less, often more, entirely of this material, after which the globular-shaped nest of root fibres, moss, bark fibres and grass is gradually built in, the spiders' webs extending for another three or four inches before being superseded by the main structure. The outside of the nest is partly covered with cob-webs or pieces of bark fibre or with both, and at times with the egg-sacs of spiders.

Birds are frequent predators of spiders and it often happens that their beaks become encumbered by webs. It is perhaps little known that birds will also eat spider egg sacs though they may actually contain a poison. In South Africa, the nests of double-collared sunbirds are made of cob-webs combined with bits of dead leaves. Moreau made the following observation:

> I have more than once seen an inhabited spider's web forming part and parcel of the nest. Whether the nest was built in the spider's web, or whether the spider found it a convenient place and selected it herself, or was brought in with a bit of web by the bird and then took up her abode and enlarged it, I cannot tell; but there the incongruous allies lived.

[123]

BULLET-PROOF VESTS

Given that spiders' silk has qualities which combine to put it above all other materials, in terms of lightness, strength and resilience, the search is now on to overcome the formidable difficulties of production on a practical scale – in particular for bullet-proof vests.

The US Defense Department is supporting classified research on the synthesis of spider silk by genetic engineering. Whereas the regular material for bullet-proof vests, *Kevlar*, can stretch up to 4 per cent before breaking, spider silk will stretch as much as 15 per cent before breaking. Silk can thus absorb more kinetic energy – from a bullet for example. Dr Stephen Fossey, one of the researchers, says that in nature, silk strands elongate in conditions of a sudden load, for example when an insect is caught, and in effect turn the prey's momentum into heat. The strands then rebound gently so as not to catapult the creature back out. This ability to dissipate energy would thus make silk ideal for ballistic protection.

The spiders in the front line are 'golden orb weavers' (*Nephila clavipes*) from Panama – big docile spiders which produce a lot of strong silk; in particular, the dragline silk is used. As much as 1,000 feet (300 metres) can be silked from a spider in one session by drawing it out on a rotating spindle. The future objective is to turn the proteins of the silk into a crystalline polymer, in large quantities. Probably this will be done, in an industrial process, by cloning the genes for silk production in spiders and by transferring them to bacteria which may then be fermented in large vats, to mass produce the new fibre.

CHAPTER EIGHT

THE DISCOVERY OF SPIDERS IN SOUTH AMERICA

For the explorer-naturalist, South America has been perhaps the most exciting land of discovery. Following epic journeys, many adventurers returned from the Amazon, and other regions, with vivid descriptions of large and remarkable species of spiders.

PUSHING BACK THE FRONTIERS

The first work on the natural history of the New World – the *Historia General y Natural de las Indias* – was by the Spanish traveller and writer, Captain Fernández de Oviedo (1478–1557). His first volume appeared in 1535 but it was not until 1855 that the entire *Historia* was published, in four volumes. In his account of the animals seen in the forest at Darien (Colombia), Oviedo described some of the spiders:

> There are spiders of marveylous bygnesse. And I have seene summe with the body and legges, bygger than a mannes hande extended every waye. And I ones sawe one of suche bygnesse, that onely her bodye was as bygge as a sparowe, and full of that laune wherof they make their webbes. This was of a dark russette coloure, with eyes greater than the eies of a sparowe. They are venemous and of terrible shape

to beholde. There are also scorpions and other suche venemous wormes.

(TRANSLATION BY RICHARD EDEN)

Don Felix de Azara (1747–1821) was sent to Paraguay as the Spanish governor from 1781 to 1801. In 1809, he published the account of his journey, in *Voyages dans l'Amérique Meridionale*. It was written with the assistance of the great French naturalist Baron C. A. Walckenaer. In his introduction, Azara wrote:

> I have spent the best part of twenty years of my life in one of the remote corners of the earth, forgotten even by my friends, without books or rational intercourse, continuously travelling through jungles, holding communications with the birds and wild beasts ... Of these I have written a history.

Azara described a number of spiders, one of which was particularly interesting:

> There is one in Paraguay who lives in a society numbering more than a hundred individuals. The body is larger than a chick pea and blackish: they construct a nest larger than a hat and suspend it from a large tree, forming a roof-like shelter. From this begins a great number of large white threads which are fifty or sixty feet long. Along them are webs, close-spaced, which trap flying ants and other insects to nourish the community of spiders. These spiders perish in the autumn, but they lay in their nest the eggs that hatch in the spring [translated from the French].

The great French naturalist of the time, Baron Walckenaer, unaware that social spiders existed, thought they must be simply a group of young *Theridion* spiders.

CHARLES DARWIN

Following the era of Spanish exploration, Charles Darwin (1809–82) visited South America as a young naturalist on the survey ship *Beagle* (1831–6). Darwin's eyes were opened by the profusion of flora and fauna in South America and on the Galapagos Islands.

> I am at present red hot with spiders, they are very interesting, and if I am not mistaken, I have already taken some new genera. I shall have a large box to send home very soon to Cambridge. (Darwin's letter to his mentor, Henslow, from the Brazilian Forest.)

During his landfall in Brazil, Darwin recorded in the *Voyage of the Beagle* (1845):

> The number of spiders in proportion to other insects is here, compared with England, very much larger. The variety of species among the jumping spiders appears almost infinite. The genus, or rather family, of *Epeira* is here characterised by many singular forms; some species have pointed coriaceous shells, others enlarged and spiny tibiae. Every path in the forest is barricaded with the strong yellow web of a species belonging to the same division with the *Epeira clavipes* of Fabricius [= *Nephila*], which was formerly said by Sloane to make, in the West Indies, webs so strong as to catch birds. A small and pretty kind of spider, with very long fore-legs, and which appears to belong to an undescribed genus [probably *Argyrodes*], lives as a parasite on almost every one of these webs. I suppose it is too insignificant to be noticed by the great *Epeira*, and is therefore allowed to prey on the minute insects, which, adhering to the lines, would otherwise be wasted. When frightened, this little spider either feigns death by extending its front legs, or suddenly drops from the web.

Near to Rio, Darwin recorded:

> I was much interested one day by watching a deadly contest
> between a *Pepsis* and a large spider of the genus *Lycosa*. The
> wasp made a sudden dash at its prey, and then flew away:
> the spider was evidently wounded, for, trying to escape, it
> rolled down a little slope, but had still strength sufficient to
> crawl into a thick tuft of grass. The wasp soon returned and
> seemed surprised at not immediately finding its victim. It
> then commenced as regular a hunt as ever did hound after
> fox; all the time rapidly vibrating its wings and antennae.
> The spider, though well concealed, was soon discovered;
> and the wasp, evidently still afraid of its adversary's jaws,
> after much manoeuvring, inflicted two stings on the under
> side of its thorax. At last, carefully examining with its
> antennae the now motionless spider, it proceeded to drag
> away the body. But I stopped both tyrant and prey.

Darwin knew about Azara's social spiders and he added:

> I found, near St. Fe Bajada, many large black spiders, with
> ruby-coloured marks on their backs, having gregarious
> habits. The webs were placed vertically, as is invariably the
> case with the genus Epeira: they were separated from each
> other by a space of about two feet, but were all attached to
> certain common lines, which were of great length, and
> extended to all parts of the community. In this manner the
> tops of some large bushes were encompassed by the united
> nets. Azara has described a gregarious spider in Paraguay,
> which Walckenaer thinks must be a Theridion, but probably
> it is an Epeira, and perhaps even the same species with mine.
> I cannot, however, recollect seeing a central nest as large as a
> hat, in which, during autumn, when the spiders die, Azara
> says the eggs are deposited. As all the spiders which I saw
> were of the same size, they must have been nearly of the
> same age. This gregarious habit, in so typical a genus as

THE DISCOVERY OF SPIDERS IN SOUTH AMERICA

Epeira, among insects which are so bloodthirsty and solitary that even the two sexes attack each other, is a very singular fact.

WEBS THIRTY FEET LONG

The spider which had attracted the attention of Azara and Darwin was probably the same as that described in *Seven eventful years in Paraguay* (1888) by G. F. Masterman, the British Ambassador. Without making any actual reference to Darwin, he wrote:

These gregarious spiders when full grown have bodies about half an inch in length, black, with the exception of a row of bright red spots, remarkably strong mandibles, and stout hairless legs nearly an inch in length. They construct in concert immense webs, often thirty feet long and eight deep, generally between two trees, and ten or twelve feet from the ground – sufficient to allow equestrians and bullock-carts to pass beneath.

In the small garden at the Legation, the spiders had stretched six of their huge nets among trees about forty feet apart; the spiders had extended two strong cables, as thick as pack-thread, to form the margin of each of the webs, and between them was a light loose net-work, imperfectly divided into webs, each presenting about a square foot of surface. Each of these sub-webs was occupied by a spider from sunset till a little after sunrise, the six [huge webs] containing about two thousand. But they often changed their location, and a double stream was always passing along the cables. They crawled over or under each other without hesitation, unlike ants, which always pause when they meet.

Soon after sunrise they left their webs, and, returning to the shade, formed two or three large masses, as big as a hat;

there they remained motionless till sunset, when the black lump crumbled to pieces – it was a curious sight to see the process, – and then, in a leisurely way, the spiders scattered themselves to their aerial fishing. The air swarmed with mosquitoes, which were caught in great numbers, but were too small game, and remained on the threads until swept away by the spiders; for they made the webs conspicuous. The larger flies, and especially the moths, were at once pounced upon and devoured by the nearest spider or several of them; and I have seen half a dozen feeding amicably together on the body of the same insect.

Masterman's conclusions were that the spiders happily work together while immature but later there arises:

> a sanguinary battle; the few survivors, all females probably, devour some of the slain and then die also. I think so, because they are all of one size in the same web, crowd together to sleep as young spiders generally do, and they disappear suddenly, leaving no stragglers behind them. I could find no remains of the slain I admit; but the activity of the swarming ants would account for that. [See social spiders, p. 94.]

PROFESSIONAL COLLECTORS

The first professional collectors in South America were Henry Walter Bates (1825–92) and Alfred Russel Wallace (1823–1913). Together, they planned to finance their expedition by selling specimens to museums and private collectors, in spite of lacking proper equipment. In 1848 the two set off and arrived in Para, at the mouth of the Amazon. They spent the first two years together. One might imagine a snippet of their conversation while they were collecting: 'My God, Bates, I do believe it's a specimen of *Avicularia*.' 'No, Wallace, a *Blondii* . . .' In 1850 they

Bird-killing spider near the river Amazon

separated: Wallace to the Rio Negro and Bates to the River Amazon. Wallace returned to England in 1852, but Bates not until 1859. Both men published full accounts of their travels, and collected and described great numbers of animals, birds, and insects which were previously unknown.

In Para, Bates did not have to go far from where he was living:

> The virgin forest is here left untouched; numerous groups of slender palms, mingled with lofty trees overrun with creepers and parasites, fill the shady glen . . . I have chanced to verify a fact relating to the habits of a large hairy spider of the genus Mygale . . . I was attracted by a movement of the monster on a tree-trunk; it was close beneath a deep crevice in the tree, across which was stretched a dense white web. The lower part of the web was broken, and two small birds, finches, were entangled in the pieces. One of them was quite dead, the other lay under the body of the spider not quite dead, and was smeared with the filthy liquor or saliva

exuded by the monster. I drove away the spider and took the birds, but the second one soon died. The fact of species of Mygale sallying forth at night, mounting trees, and sucking the eggs and young of humming-birds, has been recorded long ago by Palisot de Beauvois; but, in the absence of any confirmation, it has come to be discredited. Count Langsdorff, in his *Expedition into the Interior of Brazil*, states that he totally disbelieved the story. I found the circumstances to be quite a novelty to the residents hereabout. The Mygales are quite common insects: some species make their cells under stones, others form artistical tunnels in the earth, and some build their dens in the thatch of houses. The natives call them Aranhas carangeuijeiras, or crab-spiders. The hairs with which they are clothed come off when touched, and cause a peculiar and almost maddening irritation. The first specimen that I killed and prepared was handled incautiously, and I suffered terribly for three days afterwards. I think this is not owing to any poisonous quality residing in the hairs, but to their being short and hard, thus getting into the fine creases of the skin (*urticaria*]. Some Mygales are of immense size. One day I saw the children belonging to an Indian family, who collected for me, with one of these monsters secured by a cord around its waist, by which they were leading it as they would a dog.

Bates wrote his account of the eleven-years' adventure and travel in *The Naturalist on the River Amazons* (1863). The book's fine illustrations included one of a *Mygale avicularia* attacking finches. Bates described it as a 'bird-killing spider'. But this was by no means the earliest such illustration. Madame Merian in *Metamorphosis Insectorum Surinamensium* (1705) gave an illustrated account of a large 'mygale' dragging a hummingbird from its nest and sucking its blood. Many refused to believe the story but the spider was described by Linnaeus under the name *Mygale avicularia* [now *Avicularia avicularia*]. Today, a number of names

PLATE 17. Autumn orb-web
(*Paul Hillyard*)

PLATE 18 (*main picture*):
Autumn orb-web at night (*Araneus angulatus*) (*Paul Hillyard*)

Anticlockwise from top left:
PLATE 19. Female wolf-spider with a mass of newly hatched babies on her back in rainforest (*K. G. Preston-Mafham/Premaphotos Wildlife*)
PLATE 20. *Dinopus guatemalensis* net-casting spider poised ready with its retarius web at night in rainforest (*K. G. Preston-Mafham/Premaphotos Wildlife*)
PLATE 21. *Argyrodes elevatus* spider creeping up to feed on the prey of a giant *Nephila clavipes* female spider (*K. G. Preston-Mafham/Premaphotos Wildlife*)

Clockwise from top left
PLATE 22: Lady in Black Widow dress. PLATE 23: Spider brooch
on jumper. PLATE 24: Spider on web pendant.
PLATE 25: Embroidery – webs and leaves. PLATE 26: 'Laughing'
spider brooch. (all *Paul Hillyard*)

have become synonymous, thus: 'bird-eating' or 'bird-killing' spider = 'tarantula' = 'mygale' = the large spiders of the family Theraphosidae. Bates encountered the world's largest species of spider, known today as *Theraphosa leblondi*. He recorded:

> One very robust fellow, the Mygale Blondii, burrows into the earth, forming a broad slanting gallery, about two feet long, the sides of which he lines beautifully with silk. He is nocturnal in his habits. Just before sunset he may be seen keeping watch within the mouth of his tunnel, disappearing suddenly when he hears a heavy foot-tread near his hiding place.

TRAVELLERS' TALES

Many of the books written by naturalists and travellers in South America, during the nineteenth and early twentieth centuries, included short passages on the spiders. Mostly, compared with the descriptions of Darwin and Bates, such narratives are notable more for their entertainment value than their accuracy. In *Notes of a Botanist on the Amazon and Andes* (1908), by Richard Spruce (edited by Alfred Wallace), there is a somewhat fanciful account of poisonous spiders living at the foot of the Andes:

> After snakes, the venomous animals most to be dreaded are the large hairy spiders, especially the species of Mygale . . . all I ever heard of proved fatal except one, and that was of a woman at San Carlos, who was bitten in the heel and immediately dropped, with a shriek, as if shot. She lay at the point of death for ten days, but finally recovered. I have been bitten by spiders, but never seriously. At Tarapoto a smallish green spider abounded in the bushes, and would sometimes be lurking among my plant specimens. It bit furiously when molested, with an effect about equal to the sting of a bee.

A very fine book, *Among the Wild Tribes of the Amazon*, subtitled *An Account of Exploration and Adventure on the Mighty Amazon*, by Domville-Fife (1924), told vividly of the author's night of fear. From inside his tent, under tall trees beside the Amazon, and in the light of a bright moon, Domville-Fife became aware of a dark 'patch' moving outside. On closer investigation with the aid of a torch, the object turned out to be a large spider busy constructing its web. The web extended, in a triangle between two trees, about twenty feet apart, and included his tent! Confessing to a horror of spiders, the intrepid adventurer found the sight of this creature, silhouetted in detail through the thin canvas of the tent, chilled him greatly, in spite of the stifling heat of the tropical night. But unfortunately he could not think of a way to get rid of it. If he shot it, it would have torn the canvas and brought down the tent. A bucket of water might remove it, but perhaps send it inside! Yet he could not sleep with the spider only a foot or so from his face – although outside the tent. At last, in desperation, he roused one of the sleeping Indians in the canoe to remove the spider.

VISITING SPECIALISTS

Dr William S. Bristowe (1901–79), a unique figure in the history of British arachnology (see Chapters 2, 3, 5, 6, 8, 10) found some curious spiders in Brazil. In his paper on the 1923 Cambridge University expedition to Brazil, Bristowe wrote:

> I now pass to a most extraordinary case of mimicry. I noticed, as I thought, a very big-headed ant walking across my path, I stopped to pick it up and discovered to my surprise that it was a black Thomisid spider *which was carrying aloft by means of the two front legs of one side* a dead black ant. When I covered it with a glass-topped box, after watching it walk for about fifteen yards with a jerky rather

antlike gait, it immediately dropped its load, and I found that the ant was absolutely sucked dry, only its light and useless skeleton remaining. If this was not intentional, what was the spider doing with the empty corpse of an ant, and carried in such a position?

The case was taken up by Major R. W. G. Hingston, who led the 1929 Oxford University expedition to British Guiana (Guyana). Hingston was a meticulous observer of spiders and also ants. He said: 'What Bristowe was unable to explain, was, I am confident, not an accident but a definite device on the part of the spider to secure shelter from its enemies.' Having found a similar example in Guiana, the Major observed that the ant lay over the back of the spider and completely hid it from view.

> The spider ran about on the forest floor, stubbornly carrying the corpse on its back. When put in a glass-covered box, it ran about energetically inside but did not release the ant. Indeed it seemed to cling to it tighter than ever, as though it felt that in these strange surroundings it required all the more its peculiar disguise. Occasionally it would relax its hold for a few minutes, then take up the corpse again. When picking it up, it would carefully examine it, feeling it about in different places until it came to the back of the head. This spot, and this spot only, it would grip, before hoisting the corpse over its back.

Many years later, the same curiosity was described by P. S. Oliveira and I. Sazima (1985). The spider, *Strophius nigricans* seized a black ant from behind and simultaneously dropped in front of the ant the corpse it had been carrying. The ant struggled and bit the corpse fiercely. But as the spider's grip strengthened, it lifted the new victim aloft. When approached by other ants, the spider used the corpse aggressively as a shield to send them away.

In South America, the forests of the Guianas are fully equal to those of Brazil and the Amazon. Hingston's book of the Oxford expedition, *A Naturalist in the Guiana Forest* (1932), is full of fascinating details about spiders, especially their abilities to conceal themselves. He wrote:

> There are spiders in the forest with the strangest habits. There is a kind which hangs a trap-door shelter from the centre of its web, another which for concealment rolls itself into a kind of blanket, another which plants moss on its conical-shaped hiding-place, another which manufactures a hammock and joins forces with an army of ants to defend it, another which cuts semicircular pieces from the vegetation after the fashion of the leaf-cutting ants.

Referring to the spider with the dead ant, Hingston explained that a resemblance to ants is useful. It enables some spiders to escape their enemies and pillage the ants. In the case of this spider, its tactic seems to be to mimic an ant carrying one of its own companions, as they sometimes do. It is a kind of stalking-disguise.

Hingston pointed out: 'Spiders live continually in dread of enemies. They are always trying to keep as much as possible in concealment.' Their enemies include ants, parasitic wasps and flies, lizards and toads, and many different kinds of birds. In South America, sunbirds and spider-hunters pick them from flowers, vegetation and tree-trunks. The air-hunting birds, such as swallows, swifts, fly-catchers and drongos, catch the ballooning forms in their flight. Of the wasps and flies which feed their larvae on spiders, Hingston said:

> The toll of spiders exacted in this way is enormous. In tropical countries all round the world we continually see these predaceous hymenoptera hunting for victims or dragging them to their nests; one is always finding mud cells stuffed tight with spiders; less often we see a wasp or a fly picking its victims out of the webs. In countries infested by

these wasp–enemies, and this particularly refers to Tropical America, spiders that stretch snares across open spaces must protect themselves in some kind of way. Broadly speaking, they have learnt two methods of concealment. Either they sit outside the snare, hide themselves beneath a leaf or in some convenient nook, and keep connection with the snare, or manufacture some special concealing object which will deceive the enemy when it arrives.

CHAPTER NINE

A BRIEF HISTORY
OF SPIDER
CLASSIFICATION

Ancient Beginnings

THE GREEK PHILOSOPHER ARISTOTLE

The scientific study of spiders began with Aristotle (385–322 BC). Aristotle was the pupil of Plato, the tutor of Alexander the Great, and the founder of the Peripatetic school in Athens. He dealt with the whole range of science but saw himself largely as a classifier. We may think of him as the world's first and most advanced 'workaholic'. He realised that nature needed accurate observation instead of just simply 'common sense'. He refused to rely on the statements of others and he invariably raised interesting questions. Aristotle's writings are rich in picturesque but sometimes also fanciful material. His best known work, the nine-volume *Historia Animalium*, included many references to spiders. Darwin said that whereas Linnaeus and Cuvier had been his two gods, 'they were mere schoolboys to old Aristotle'.

Aristotle was the first to attempt a classification of animals. He arranged them according to the colour of their blood (red or white). White-blooded animals were separated into four groups, Crustacea, Mollusca, Testacea (e.g. oysters) and Insecta (including spiders). He was a careful observer of spiders but it is difficult today to identify his species: 'Of spiders and phalangia there are many species.' He arranged them into two categories: the harmless or common-spiders, most of which spin conspicuous webs, and the *Phalangia* or venom spiders. Unfortunately the distinction between them is rather vague. He tells us: 'The smooth spider is much less prolific than the phalangium or hairy spider'; and also: 'Some are more skilful and more resourceful than others.' Often, however, Aristotle was surprisingly accurate. He found that females seem more numerous than males, and he described spider courtship for the first time: 'The female takes hold of the web at the middle and gives a pull, and the male gives a counter pull; this operation they repeat until they are close together.'

On reproduction in common-spiders, he mentioned the meadow spider, which 'lays its eggs into a web, of which one half is attached to itself; on this the parent broods until the eggs are hatched'. Probably this species is a kind of wolf spider, *Lycosa* or *Pardosa*, whose females construct portable egg sacs. Aristotle's writings were sometimes wrong – it is said for example, that spiders breed by uniting their rears and that they reproduce through grubs or larvae. However, a number of such errors are probably due to mistakes in translation, and some have since been repeated many times. In his *Génération des ánimaux*, Aristotle clearly stated that spiders *do not* have larvae.

On the subject of web-form, Aristotle distinguished those which produce coarse and irregular webs from the orb-weavers with their much finer workmanship. He wrote:

There are two kinds of spiders which spin thick webs, the larger and the smaller. The one has long legs and lies in wait hanging upside down on its web [probably *Pholcus*]. Because of its large size, it cannot readily conceal itself so it keeps underneath, so that its prey may not be frightened off, but may strike upon the web's upper surface. The less awkward one [probably *Tegenaria*] keeps watch from the top of the web, using a hole for a lurking place.

Of the spider which spins the delicate orb-web (*Araneus* or *Tetragnatha*), Aristotle described it as 'pre-eminently clever and artistic'. He gave the first ever account of web-building and used the language of human weaving:

> It first weaves a thread stretching to all the exterior ends of the future web: then from the centre, which it hits upon with great accuracy; it weaves the whole together. It sleeps and stores its food away from the centre, but it is at the centre that it keeps watch for its prey. Then when any creature touches the web and the centre is set in motion, it first wraps the creature round with threads, until it renders it helpless, then lifts it and carries it off, and, if it happens to be hungry, sucks out the life juices but if it be not hungry, it first mends any damage done [cf. Fabre, page 84] and then hastens again to its quest of prey. If something comes meanwhile into the net, the spider makes first for the centre and then goes back to its entangled prey as from a fixed starting-point.
>
> If anyone injures a portion of the web, it resumes weaving at sunrise or at sunset, because it is mainly at these periods that creatures are caught. It is the female that does the weaving and catching, but the male takes a share of the booty ... Spiders can spin webs from the time of their birth, not from their interior, as a superfluity or excretion, as Democritus avers [correctly], but off their body as a kind of tree-bark, like the creatures that shoot out their hairs, for instance the porcupine. The creature can attack animals larger than itself, and enwrap them with its threads: in other words, it will attack a small lizard, run round and draw threads about its mouth until it closes the mouth up; then it comes up and bites it.

Aristotle referred to 'those phalangia which spin webs' and probably he had in mind the one really venomous spider in the region – *Latrodectus*. In the ninth volume, which may not be purely Aristotelian – it is said:

> Of the venomous phalangia there are two; one that resembles the so-called wolf spider, small, speckled, and tapering to a point; it moves with leaps, from which habit it is nicknamed 'the flea' [probably a harmless jumping spider]: the other kind is large, black in colour, with long front legs; it is heavy in its movements, walks slowly, is not very strong, and never leaps. Of these, the small one weaves no web, and the large one weaves a rude and poorly built one on the ground or on dry stone walls. It always builds its web over hollow places inside of which it keeps a watch on the end-threads, until some creature gets into the web and begins to struggle, when out the spider pounces [probably *Segestria*].
>
> The phalangia lay their eggs in a sort of basket which they have woven, and brood over it until the eggs are hatched. These phalangia, when they grow to full size, very often envelop the mother phalangium and eject and kill her; and not seldom they kill the father-phalangium as well if they catch him [inaccurate]: for, by the way, he has the habit of co-operating with the mother in the hatching. The brood of a single phalangium is sometimes three hundred in number. The spider attains its full growth in about four weeks.

The Greek Philostratus, according to Ian Beavis, had some quaint misconceptions. Philostratus believed that spiders have two separate kinds of web: broad and open ones for use in the summer, and enclosed ones for the winter – spiders not only spin webs to catch prey but also to keep themselves warm. Philostratus also mentioned the spiders' habit of using silk threads to let themselves down to the ground and climb back up to their previous position.

THE ROMAN EMPIRE – PLINY THE ELDER

Diodorus Siculus, or Diodor of Sicily, recorded (*c.* 60 BC) in *Bibliotheca Historica*, a dreadful plague of spiders in Abyssinia. The land was at the time of writing deserted and barren, but it had been 'rich in fair pastures', and well populated. In the space of one season, however, all this was changed by climatic disturbances which caused great numbers of spiders to spring up – 'regio phalangiis infesta' – they were so dangerous and their bites so dreaded that the inhabitants were compelled to move to other lands.

Pliny the Elder (AD 23–79) was an assiduous collector of knowledge about plants and animals. He brought together facts and fables, superstitions and anecdotes, true and false, in one great 37-volume compendium, the *Historia Naturalis*. His encyclopaedic but indiscriminate compilation of material unfortunately did not distinguish fact from fiction and he liked to embroider both with his own fantasies; although entertaining, much of it was useless.

Pliny said that to observe spiders handling large prey is a spectacle worthy of the amphitheatre. He described the method used by a spider to defeat a snake: The spider is poised in her web in a tree while the snake lies coiled in the shade beneath. From her aerial position the spider launches an attack by throwing herself upon the head of the snake and piercing its brain with her fangs. 'Such is the shock,' relates Pliny, 'that the creature will hiss from time to time, and then seized with vertigo, coil round and round, unable to break the web of the spider. The scene ends only with its death.'

Pliny went on to describe the spider as a ferocious creature which is most dangerous in the summer. He also stated that spiders couple backwards and produce maggots which look like eggs, take three days to hatch, and reach full size in 28 days. In other words, Pliny copied Aristotle without taking the trouble to look for himself. As often, he misread Aristotle's passage concerning the female who spins the web while the male has a share in what is caught. Pliny has it that the female does the spinning while the male does the hunting. On the diversity of spiders, Pliny added few new observations beyond the writings of Aristotle: 'There are several kinds, but they need not be described as they are well known.'

In the works of Aristotle and Pliny, as well as in those of some of their contemporaries, a number of names were used which are still in use today: *Lycosa*, *Tetragnatha*, *Dysdera*, *Tarantula* and *Phalangium* [now a 'harvest-spider']. However, it is not really possible to match their vague descriptions – they did not have our concept of species – with today's classification.

Europe from the Fifteenth to the start of the Twentieth Century

After the fall of Rome in AD 395, there followed a period of more than 1,000 years, the 'Dark Ages', during which little was apparently written on spiders. The two great authors, Aristotle and Pliny, continued to be the principal authorities on natural history centuries after their works were written. But of the two, the writings of Aristotle had become badly distorted by the Middle Ages because of translation from Greek into Arabic and then Latin. In fact it was Pliny who was recognised as the foremost authority throughout mediaeval times. His mixture of truth and fiction fitted well with the many travellers' tales and the early printed books which were generally of a very uncritical character. Aristotle's *Historia Animalium* was not fully appreciated again until the sixteenth century when, following the fall of Constantinople, his Greek manuscripts were released and could be accurately translated into Latin, e.g. the translation of Theodore of Gaza (Venice, 1476).

[143]

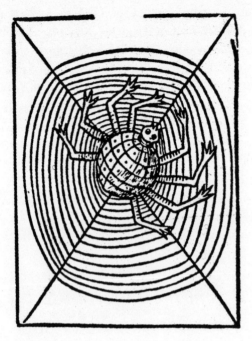

Early illustration of a spider on its orb-web

An early work on natural history was that of the German naturalist, Konrad von Magenberg who wrote the *Buch der Natur* (1475). Von Magenberg followed Pliny in stating that spiders originated from decaying matter, that they grew from seeds which were carried by the rays of the sun, and that if a person swallowed a spider these seeds would remain in his or her saliva.

The first important biological work in English: *The Noble Lyfe & Natures of Man, of Bestes, Serpentys, Fowles & Fisshes yt be Most Knowen*, was written in 1521 by Laurence Andrewes. It has a number of references to spiders. It was derived from *Hortus Sanitatus* (1491) which contains one of the first illustrations of a spider – in an orb-web (see Spiders in art, p. 34). According to Jones–Walters, only two copies of *The Noble Lyfe* exist. Andrewes wrote:

The spynner or spyder is so named because it spinneth a gret dele of webbe or threde, and it worketh always and whan it hathe all done with a blast of wynde it tereth asonder and all the labour is lost that it hath do, the spider hathe many fete at leste VI or VIII and it sitteth in the myddes of the webbe redy to take suche flyes and vermyn as cometh in it, and their moistour they sucke and therby they lette, whan they engender the female lieth under with her bely upward, and they lay egges and of those egges come yonge spynners whiche spynne incontinent.

Plini with Diascorides tellefieth that the whyte and pure webbe is very soverayne to many things, and specially to be layde to a fresche wounde for it stauncheth the blode, it kepeth it from swelling, from filyng, and it comfortheth the wounde.

Plinius, for the stinge or bitte of the spinner is gode the brayne of a capon with a lytell peper dronke in swete wyne. Also the talowe of a lamme is gode to be dronke with swete wyne for the bitte of the spinner. Also flies brayed in peces and layde to the bitte of the spynner swageth the payne and draweth oute all the venym.

Eventually, the traditional adherence to Ancient Authority was dropped in preference to the evidence of one's own eyes. Slowly at first in the sixteenth century, and then more rapidly in the seventeenth and eighteenth centuries, the study of spiders was 'reborn' as the craft of printing spread across Europe. Entrenched beliefs about spiders such as the dangers of tarantism (see page 55) were questioned and natural phenomena such as gossamer (see page 29) were debated.

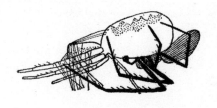

[145]

THE FIRST SPECIALISTS ON SPIDERS

According to Theodore Savory, Caelius Secundus Curio wrote a book, the first ever on spiders alone, of 88 pages called *Araneus, seu de Providentiae Dei*. It was published in Basel in 1544. Presented as a sermon, the facts on spiders, both true and false, were taken from the writings of Pliny and were used as evidence for the wisdom and goodness of the Creator. Another, Ulysses Aldrovandrus, like Pliny, attempted to assemble all that had been written before on spiders. In his comprehensive treatise *De Animalibus Insectis*, published in 1602 at Bologna, the chapter 'De Araneis' described 28 species but unfortunately none of the woodcuts can be identified today. He also wrote about tarantism and the tarantella.

TOPSELL AND MOUFFET

The most entertaining accounts of spiders from early times are to be found in *The History of Four-footed Beasts and Serpents*, written by the Rev E. Topsell and published in 1607. Topsell may claim to have been the first to produce an illustration of a spider which can be recognised today as that of a particular species (*Araneus diadematus*). However, it is said that his work

owed much to the uncompleted *Historia Animalium* of the Swiss Konrad Gesner (1515–65), one of the most learned naturalists of the sixteenth century. Unfortunately Topsell continued to follow established opinion (Greco-Roman) when he said that spiders were lowly creatures born of inanimate matter: 'It is manifest that spiders are bred of some aereall seeds putrefied from filth and corruption, because even the newest houses the first day they are whited will have spiders and cobwebs in them.' Of 'spiders that are hurtful', he asserted: 'Grevious symptomes follow the bitings of the Phalangium, for there followes a mighty swelling on the part bitten, the knees grow weak, the heart trembles, the forces fail, and oft-times death suceeds.'

The second edition of Topsell's *History* (1658) incorporated an English translation (*The Theater of Insects*) of the long-delayed *Insectorum Theatrum* of Dr Thomas Mouffet. Mouffet had taken over the 'disorganised' *Insectorum* from Thomas Penny following Penny's death in 1588. According to Mouffet's introduction, he put the work in order, gave it literary style, cut out 'more than a thousand tautologies and trivialities' and added over 150 illustrations. In doing so he obscured or destroyed much of the work of Penny, the first English entomologist.

Mouffet's *Insectorum Theatrum* was completed in 1589 but not published until 1634, some 30 years after his death. It contained several chapters on spiders and he laid emphasis on their God-given qualities: 'To praise the spider as I ought, I shall first set before you the riches of its body, then of its fortune, lastly of its minde.' Of the house-spider he wrote lovingly:

> As if Nature had appointed not only to make it round like the Heavens, but with rays like the stars, as if they were alive. The skin of it is so soft, smooth, polished and neat, that she precedes the softest skind Mayds, and the daintiest and most beautiful strumpets. She hath fingers that the most gallant virgins desire to have theirs like them, long, slender, round, of exact feeling, that there is no man, not any creature that can compare with her ... Who would not admire so great force, so sharp and hard bitings, and almost incredible strength in so small a body, having neither bones, nerves, flesh and hardly any skin? This cannot proceed from its body, but its spirit; or rather God himself.

Mouffet also praised the perfection of the orb-web and suggested that Euclid could have learnt his geometry from it. He knew all about the craze of tarantism in Italy (see page 55). He was well educated, but had little in common with the next generation of naturalists.

THE SCIENTIFIC AGE BEGINS

In England, scientific advances really took off in the second half of the seventeenth century. Progress was greatly boosted by the development of the microscope – in England by Robert Hooke and in Holland by Antonie van Leeuwenhoek who made a visit to London in 1666. Hooke's book *Micrographia* (1665) was remarkable for its original and accurate figures of the most minute bodies. It included only a few spiders but he described two of their relatives, the 'shepherd spider' (a harvestman), and a 'crab-like insect' (a pseudoscorpion).

MARTIN LISTER AND JOHN RAY

An enthusiastic group of scholars during this period included John Ray, the famous naturalist, and Martin Lister, the first British arachnologist. Both were students at Cambridge but they met in France and both became leading members of the Royal Society. The two had a long dialogue on spiders (despite Ray's professed horror of them) and both were particularly interested in gossamer and aeronautic dispersal. Ray's *Historia Insectorum* (1710) had 30 pages of spiders based on the work of Lister.

Martin Lister (1638–1712) was a doctor and it may be said that he began the tradition which continues to this day, at least in Britain, that arachnologists are doctors, clergymen or schoolmasters – anything but professional zoologists. Lister's fine, illustrated *Tractatus De Araneis* (1678) was published in Latin and for that very reason it suffered from years of neglect – we have had to wait until 1992 for the first translation into English (by Parker and Harley).

In his preface, Lister recalled that ten years previously he had studied most of the 'insects' of Britain. On spiders in particular he had spent much time on field work in Lincolnshire – 'not merely hours or even days but whole months'. He went so far as to say, after reviewing his notes during the following winter: 'the other insects are less important than the family of spiders, both by reason of the number of species and their mode of existence'. He asserted confidently: 'I do not want anyone to suppose that I have described every single species but I will say that it is not easy to find in this island any new species that I have failed to describe.'

Because of his confidence, Lister would have been surprised that his total of 38 species of British spiders (including 3 harvestmen and a mite) was to rise to over 300 in *The Spiders of Great Britain and Ireland* by John Blackwall (1861–4); and to its present-day total of around 640. However, notwithstanding his paucity of species, Lister's *Tractatus* is a milestone – the first book to be written exclusively on British spiders. And because of its accurate descriptions and drawings, the spiders are easily identifiable today. They are species typical of meadow and woodland, and interestingly, the large Tegenarias, familiar to the British today as house spiders, are conspicuous by their absence.

Lister classified spiders by characters such as, on the one hand: 'Of spiders weaving linen-like webs, with the threads of the web densely interwoven in the fashion of a veil or piece of cloth'; and on the other hand: 'Of hunting spiders, namely those which pursue flies in the open without a contrivance of mesh or web.' In fact, he came close to devising a modern system of classification. He did not name the species but numbered them, from *Titulus 1* to *Titulus 38*. For example, *Titulus 2* is the garden spider, *Araneus diadematus*. Had he actually used names, Lister might today be recognised as the founder of taxonomy. His *Tractatus* pre-dated the *Systema Naturae* of Linnaeus by 80 years.

Lister's preface showed his understanding of taxomony:

> I am arranging the animals of the individual genera in species. The obvious utility of this arrangement is that if hereafter other scholars' experiments produce fresh information, this may be safely included in the present arrangement and each detail may be assigned to its correct place. In the meantime, it will be more than enough for me that I have been the first to clarify the nature of these particular animals to this generation's students of natural history. Those who in the future undertake a like task will at least understand the extent of my labour and will see that to understand such minute details, even in outline, constitutes something of an achievement.

PIONEERING EUROPEANS

Lister, Ray and Hooke were British contemporaries of the two pioneering Dutch microscopists, Antonie van Leeuwenhoek (1632–1723) and Jan Swammerdam (1637–80). Swammerdam made a number of original observations about spiders – he discovered that jumping spiders are long-sighted and that female wolf-spiders attach themselves to their egg-cocoons. In his most important book, the *Bybel der Natuur af Historie der Insecten*, published after his death in 1737, he classified spiders together with slugs and leeches on the grounds that they emerge from the egg with the same form as when fully grown. In spite of making such a strange alliance, Swammerdam was the first to describe the function of the palps of male spiders in transferring spermatozoa.

Leeuwenhoek in 1701, using his own microscope, presented

a paper entitled 'Concerning spiders, their way of killing prey, spinning their webs, generation etc' to the *Philosophical Transactions* of the Royal Society. In it he showed for the first time the three claws at the end of each leg (in web spinners). He drew the mouthparts including the poison fangs and revealed the opening of the poison–duct and the accessory teeth. He drew the four pairs of eyes and made the first description of the spinning organs. He kept spiders in captivity and, fixing a garden spider upside down, was able to draw out silk threads from its spinnerets.

In Britain, the successor to Lister was Eleazar Albin (1713–59). Albin was an artist who lived in London; his book, *A Natural History of Spiders and Other Curious Insects* was published in 1736. He illustrated nearly 150 spiders but most are difficult to identify today and many simply are colour variations of the same species. Like Lister, he was content to number them rather than give names. Probably the most interesting parts of Albin's book were those written by others. Dr Richard Mead contributed a section on the phenomenon of the Tarantella, entitled 'Of the Tarantula', and there was a section entitled 'Microscopical Observations on the Crab Spider and the Jumping Spider By the late Dr Hooke, F.R.S.'

SPIDERS GET SCIENTIFIC NAMES

The modern system of biological classification, based on pairs of latinised names (the binomial system) was founded by the Swedish botanist Carl von Linné (Carolus Linnaeus, 1707–78). The 10th edition (1758) of his *Systema Naturae*, in which the binomial system was introduced, has been chosen by the International Commission on Zoological Nomenclature as the starting point of animal taxonomy. However, the starting point for spiders is accepted as being different. Although Linnaeus included 37 spider species, the beginning of spider nomenclature is taken to be the excellent *Svenska Spindlar* or *Aranei Suecici* (Swedish Spiders) by Carl Clerck, a 48-year-old Stockholm tax collector.

Svenska Spindlar was actually the first zoological work to use the binomial system. When it was published in 1757, the 10th edition of the *Systema Naturae* was a year behind but had gone too far to include the Clerckian names. Clerck featured 68 species and his descriptions were superior to those of Linnaeus. Thus for many species, Clerck's names have come to be used in preference. For example, *Araneus diadematus* Clerck, 1757 is used in preference to *Aranea diadema* Linnaeus, 1758 (by convention the author's name and date follows the species name). In fact, the zoological congress at Moscow, 1892, formally rejected the Clerckian names but the supporters (the 'Clerckists') kept opposing the ruling until they overturned it at the meeting of the International Commission in Paris, 1948.

AFTER LINNAEUS – FROM SWEDEN TO FRANCE

Until the end of the eighteenth century, spiders were considered to be nothing more than wingless insects. About 500 species were placed in a single genus – *Aranea* or *Araneus*. Spiders were first classified, in their own family, the Araneides, by a pair of French naturalists who sorted them out according to their appearance, habits and web design. Pierre Latreille (1762–1833), the first author to establish a set of spider genera, was also the world's first to hold a professorship of entomology. His work on world-wide classification, at the Académie des Sciences in Paris, culminated in *Les Crustaces, les Arachnides, les Insectes distribués en familles naturelles* (1829). The great Baron, Charles Walckenaer (1771–1852) continued Latreille's work and, over a period of a decade, produced the four-volume *Histoire naturelle des Insectes Aptères*. It occupies a permanent place in classification because it introduced many names of genera which are still recognised today.

GERMANY COMES TO THE FORE

Following Latreille and Walckenaer, the headquarters of spider classification shifted from France to Germany. Carl Hahn (1786–1836) wrote two great works, the *Monographie der Spinnen*, which was devoted entirely to spiders, and *Die Arachniden*. Only two volumes of the latter were completed at the time of his death but fortunately, Carl Ludwig Koch (1778–1857) went on to complete, between 1836 and 1848, the magnificent 16 volumes of *Die Arachniden*. In contrast to the French books with their terse descriptions and infrequent illustrations, *Die Arachniden*'s 563 exquisite plates captured the attention of zoologists everywhere. Its major shortcoming, realised later, was the lack of a natural arrangement and classification. However, it was the first to separate a newly established class, the Arachnida, from the Insecta. The son, Ludwig Carl Koch (1825–1908) inherited his father's enthusiasm for spiders. He worked on spiders from all over the world, his best known work being the great *Die Arachniden Australiens*.

JOHN BLACKWALL IN ENGLAND

In Britain, after a fallow period of 140 years since Lister's book of 1678, John Blackwall was the first of a succession of spider enthusiasts, each of them personally acquainted with his successors in the next generation. Thus the Rev. O. Pickard-Cambridge (1828–1917), who had been guided by Blackwall, in turn assisted his nephew, F. O. Pickard-Cambridge (1860–1905), A. R. Jackson (1877–1944) and a number of others.

Born in Manchester, John Blackwall (1790–1881) retired

from his father's business at the age of 44 and lived at Hendre House, Llanrwst, North Wales. His papers on spiders, from Britain and around the world, spanned a period of almost half a century. Blackwall revised all previous classifications, taking into account the arrangement of the eyes and the form of the male palpal organ. Despite using only a single lens instead of a microscope, he discovered that many species are really quite tiny – less than one tenth of an inch (3 mm) long – the reason why they were previously unknown. Lister's total of 34 British species soon became hopelessly out of date. The total rose to 304 in Blackwall's famous, two-volume work, *A History of the Spiders of Great Britain and Ireland* (1860–4). Unfortunately, because of the secluded life he lived at Llanrwst, Blackwall had little contact with contemporary experts on the Continent of Europe, such as Koch, Keyserling and Hahn. This led to him describing as new species, many spiders which had already been described on the Continent.

The Ray Society of London originally contacted Blackwall to produce his comprehensive book in conjunction with Robert Templeton of Belfast, though Templeton's name was later dropped. Today it is not clear who is responsible for all of the excellent illustrations. The 500 in the *History* are thought to have been drawn by three individuals. Seventeen of the twenty-nine plates are by the principal artist, Tuffen West; two plates bear the name of A. Hollick; and ten are anonymous. Because Tuffen West became ill, a confusion arose over some of the type specimens of spiders and O. Pickard-Cambridge was asked to help. He may also have been the artist responsible for the ten anonymous plates.

OCTAVIUS PICKARD-CAMBRIDGE

The Rev Octavius Pickard-Cambridge (1828–1917) was rector and squire of the village of Bloxworth in Dorset, as was his father and grandfather before him. In all, the three served the church from 1780 to 1917. Octavius Pickard-Cambridge became parish priest in 1860 and his light pastoral duties left him plenty of time for the study of spiders. His son Arthur wrote in the *Memoir* of Octavius: 'From the time of his entry into the Rectory until his death, my father lived the uneventful life of a country parson.'

Partly because of Bloxworth's location, among the peaceful downs and heaths of southern England, the home of Pickard-Cambridge is modestly famous as the spiritual shrine of British arachnology. There were, and still are, few collecting grounds in Britain better than the Bloxworth district, which is full of the choicest spots for the love of nature, such as Bere Wood. But Pickard-Cambridge did not stay at home; his visits to Europe, Egypt, Syria and the Holy Land were memorable journeys. And he knew all of the great European arachnologists of the period: John Blackwall, Ludwig Koch, Eugène Simon and others.

At the Rectory it was an idyllic life, and the parson was an enthusiastic and warm-hearted man. He wrote an enormous number of papers on subjects ranging from Megalithic remains and meteorology, to ornithology and entomology. In spite of his spirituality, he was an early believer in evolution and he corresponded a good deal with Charles Darwin and Alfred Russel Wallace. The latter visited Bloxworth several times. In 1874 Darwin and Pickard-Cambridge had a dialogue on the subject of male spiders and their small size compared with females. Both were also interested in the peculiar appearance of some males – which could be of no 'imaginable use' to that sex.

Spiders were Pickard-Cambridge's greatest love, and his

first paper was entitled: *Abstinence of a Spider*. Altogether he wrote 165 papers on worldwide Arachnida, in every year from 1852 to 1914, except 1864 and 1865 when he was abroad. He described the spiders in the great series *Biologia Centrali-Americana* and in Moggridge's *Harvesting Ants and Trapdoor Spiders* (1873). He was elected to the Royal Society in 1887 in recognition of his outstanding record. His last paper, at the age of 85, was beautifully illustrated with his own drawings.

Pickard-Cambridge is perhaps best remembered for the modestly titled book *The Spiders of Dorset* (1879–81), which in fact covered the whole country. In the words of his son:

> It was characteristic of my father that the species not found in the county [of Dorset] were relegated to an appendix. This caused some inconvenience to those who were not privileged to live there, and the mistake, if it was one, was not repeated in later works.

British spider study advanced greatly in Pickard-Cambridge's time. From Blackwall's 304 species in 1864, the number rose in successive lists published by Pickard-Cambridge to 540 when he retired. Today, the British spider list contains 110 species which were described by him as new to science – many consider him to be the greatest British arachnologist of all time.

EUGÈNE SIMON AND HIS WORLD CLASSIFICATION

The greatest French arachnologist was Eugène Simon (1848–1924). Born to a wealthy Parisian family and educated at the Sorbonne, Eugène followed his father as a 'fervent admirateur des choses de la nature'. Young Eugène made frequent visits with his father to the botanical gardens and he spent hours copying the plates from Cuvier's *Règne Animal*. He soon realised that no books in French were written exclusively on the subject of spiders, so he set about the task without delay. At the age of 16, Simon wrote the first edition of his *Histoire Naturelle des Araignées* (1864), a worldwide classification.

Simon's great ambition was to describe the nation's Arachnida and so, accordingly, the first volume of *Les Arachnides de France* was published in 1874. The quality of this work was immediately obvious and in the following year, at the age of 27, Simon became president of the Société entomologique de France. Among his varied interests, he was also a recognised authority on humming-birds. Many eminent colleagues were welcomed to his home at 16 Villa Said, near the Bois de Boulogne – a shrine to French arachnology.

In his enthusiastic search for spiders he became a frequent traveller to Mediterranean lands, and later to tropical countries, usually in the company of his wife. Also, whenever possible, he carefully arranged to be in a different part of France at the best season. He found many new spiders which had been previously overlooked. *Saitis barbipes*, a pretty jumping spider, common in France, had to wait for Simon to discover it.

After the fifth volume of *Les Arachnides de France* (1884), he returned to the *Histoire Naturelle des Araignées*, the second edition of which appeared in two volumes (1892–1903). It was the product of many collections made on journeys to exotic parts of the world together with great quantities of material sent to him by other collectors. As a comprehensive guide to the spiders of the world, this second edition is, even today, the most useful of all – though its illustrations are crude and infrequent.

Without pause, and following all the considerable changes in classification which he himself had made, Simon began a revision of *Les Arachnides de France* – the sixth volume. It appeared in five parts from 1914 to 1937 (with the help of Lucien Berland after Simon's death) and remains to this day the best single guide to the spiders of the Mediterranean Region.

Simon's industry was legendary, as was his memory. He never discarded a specimen and never stopped collecting. At the end, his collection numbered over 20,000 glass tubes, with some species represented by hundreds of specimens. It is fair to say that his labelling was not good but his memory was so sharp that he could recall the collection of a single specimen, perhaps last seen twenty years earlier.

More than any previous authority on classification, Simon took into account all the various points of difference and resemblance available to him – e.g. size, behaviour, mouth-parts, spinning organs, respiration organs, sex organs, eyes, etc. His classification remained the consensus view until the late twentieth century when the old belief in a separate lineage based on the possession of cribellate silk was discontinued. Theodore Savory recorded a fitting tribute to Simon: 'He had come to arachnology as a boy of 16 and found it in an elementary and chaotic state; he left it securely founded on logical principles of his own.'

THE END OF AN ERA

During the eighteenth and nineteenth centuries a huge amount of collecting and classifying took place. Also many synonyms were created (one species with many names) – mostly by authors with little knowledge of the work of others. Theodore Savory suggested that for every 'new' spider of the period there were as many as six different names. Eugène Simon helped to sort this out. Around 1900, when the *Histoire Naturelle des Araignées* was published, about 15,000 genuine species of spiders in the world had been described and arranged in about 60 families. Almost 100 years later, the number has grown to over 34,000 species in 105 families. Present estimates of the true number of species living in the world are as large as 170,000 (Coddington and Levi).

CHAPTER TEN

THE GOLDEN AGE OF SPIDEROLOGY

Experts on spiders are usually thought of as eccentric. In the past there were some colourful characters who seemed to live up to that image. But others were quiet and studious. Let us say that many were brilliant in their own way. Almost all of them were men. Their 'golden age' was perhaps the period spanning the nineteenth and early twentieth centuries. This was the time when individuals wrote about their discoveries of nature in a charming and readable way. In the present age of academic biology, centred on universities and institutions, that charm has mostly gone.

NICHOLAS HENTZ

In America, Nicholas Marcellus Hentz (1797–1856) was the first to pursue spiders seriously. Born in Versailles, his family fled to America in 1816, at the time of the fall of Napoleon. Nicholas Hentz made his living as a teacher of French and painting. When he began the study of spiders he found an almost entirely unexplored field. Before his time, no texts relating to North American spiders had been published.

Hentz became known as 'the weird spider man', not because of his fascination with spiders but because of his morbid spirituality. Without warning, in the midst of a conversation, he would fall to his knees, raise his eyes to the heavens, spend several minutes in prayer, and then resume the conversation.

Hentz was undoubtedly eccentric and he also became addicted to a daily injection of morphine, which he claimed was to soothe a nervous condition.

After his marriage in Massachusetts in 1824, Hentz and his wife moved to North Carolina and later to Covington, Kentucky, where he became headmaster at a female seminary. In fact he moved quite frequently, and always to girl's schools. He had very little contact with other spider specialists though he did receive help from John Abbot, the naturalist from Georgia famed for his artwork. Hentz was himself a painter of miniatures, and he found spiders worthy of meticulous work, though he was criticised, somewhat unfairly, for painting their legs too short.

His first paper on spiders was published in 1821: 'A notice concerning the spider whose web is used in medicine (*Tegenaria medicinalis*).' But it was not until almost 20 years after his death that his complete works were published, by the Boston Society of Natural History, under the title *The Spiders of the United States* (1875). Additional notes on spiders were supplied by J. H. Emerton and its introduction was by the eldest son, Charles Hentz, who attested to his father's curious behaviour. Unfortunately, the Boston Society recorded some years later that after receiving Hentz's collection of spiders it had been almost entirely destroyed. His published illustrations remain as the only type specimens.

The following is an extract of a description from *The Spiders of the United States* ('wolf spiders', *Lycosa* spp., were one of his favourite groups):

It is extremely difficult to distinguish the different species of Lycosa, owing to the infinite varieties in colors, marking and size. Future writers will probably clear the confusion which I boast not of having removed during twenty years of studious attention to this genus.

1. LYCOSA FATIFERA

Description. Bluish black; cephalothorax deeper in color at the sides; cheliceres covered with rufous hairs and with a red elevation on their external side near the base; one of the largest species.

Observations. This formidable species dwells in holes ten or twelve inches in depth, in light soil, which it digs itself; for the cavity is always proportionate to the size of the spider. The orifice of the hole has a ring, made chiefly of silk, which prevents the soil from falling in when it rains. This Lycosa, probably as large as the *Tarantula* of the South of Europe, is common in Massachusetts; but we have not heard of serious accidents produced by its bite. Its poison, however, must be of the same nature and as virulent. The reason perhaps why nothing is said of its venom, is, that so very few instances can have occurred of its biting anybody. All persons shun spiders, and these shun mankind still more. Moreover, their cheliceres cannot open at an angle which can enable them to grasp a large object. Without denying its power to poison, which it certainly has, it is well to expose popular errors, such as that of the Romans in regard to the bite of the shrew, which it is now proved cannot open its mouth wide enough to bite at all. This spider, when captured, shows some combativeness, and has uncommon tenacity of life. It is a laborious task to dig down its deep hole with the care necessary not to injure it. I have at times introduced a long slender straw downward, till I could feel a resistance, and also the struggle of the tenant; and I could perceive that it bit the straw. In one or two instances, by lifting the straw gradually, I brought up the enraged spider still biting the inert instrument of its wrath. It probably lives many years. A piceous variety is found in Alabama, with the first two joints of the legs, pectus and abdomen yellowish underneath, or lighter in color.

Habitat. Massachusetts, North Alabama.

HENRY C. McCOOK

The Reverend Doctor Henry C. McCook (1837–1911) was arguably the greatest and most original author on spiders the world has ever known. His life seems to have been followed as a kind of mission. On the morning after his death, a leading Philadelphia newspaper mourned the loss of this remarkable man. He had been a powerful preacher and was one of the 'fighting McCooks' of the Civil War. His works on natural history were described as the happy combination of scientific accuracy and the kind of charm normally found only in romances.

Henry McCook was born in New Lisbon, Ohio. He attended Jefferson College, Canonsburg, Pennsylvania, and finally studied at the Western Theological Seminary, Allegheny. In 1861 he married Emma Herter. During the Civil War he was a First Lieutenant and the Chaplain for the Illinois Volunteers. In 1870 he became the minister at the Tabernacle Presbyterian Church in Philadelphia. He was an active theologian and an ardent patriot. His studies on spiders, and also ants, began about 1873. He entered the American Entomological Society in 1877 and became president from 1898 to 1900. He was an honorary member of the British Association for the Advancement of Science. In a busy life, he wrote of the difficulties faced by a field naturalist:

> The duties of my calling in a large city have held me rigorously away from the open country except during two months of the year. Summer vacations, and such leisure hours as a most busy life would allow, have been given to the pleasant task of following my little friends.

McCook's great work was his three-volume *American Spiders and their Spinning Work – A Natural History of the Orb-weaving Spiders of the United States, with special regard to their Industry and*

Habits. Packed with original observations and abundant illustrations selected from thousands of field sketches, this work has more appeal than any other on spiders, before or since. McCook was the author, the artist and the publisher. His three volumes were entitled *Snares and Nests* (1889), *Motherhood and Babyhood: Life and Death* (1890), and *Biological Notes: Description of Species and Plates* (1894). In the Preface he explained why he was the publisher:

> In order to give my investigations to the public in any form that would satisfy me, I have been compelled to undertake the entire burden and expense of publication. Few things could be more inconvenient and distasteful than the business details thus imposed; but I have accepted them as a part of the sacrifice required of one who, as a prophet of the mysteries of Nature, feels called to declare, at whatever cost, the truths known to him.

The edition was limited to 250 copies.

American Spiders and their Spinning Work is clearly a labour of love which flourished partly because it was free of the need to make a profit. The illustrations are beautifully drawn and the writing is charming, although, in the style of the period, unashamedly anthropomorphic. McCook delighted in anecdotes which refuted the opinions of others. For example, he cited the case, mentioned by Romanes, of a web-spinning spider which had lost five of its legs and so could only spin very imperfectly. It was claimed to have changed its habits to those of a hunting spider which catches its prey by stalking. McCook asserted:

> My observations are wholly contradictory of this. I have placed on my vines an Epeira domiciliorum [=*Neoscona benjamina*] that had lost all the legs on one side, and found it to weave a serviceable web, although necessarily somewhat imperfect. It hung upon its snare and trapped flies with fair success.

Using an ancedote of a yacht and its skipper on the St Lawrence River, McCook answered the question which puzzles many people: 'Where do webs come from?' The skipper had complained that every morning he had to brush away webs from his vessel. He never could make out where they all came from, or how they got aboard the ship. McCook explained:

> I was able to solve the man's perplexity . . . I examined the under parts of the railing and the cornices of projecting parts of the deck, and discovered a large number of orbweavers, mostly Epeira strix [=*Larinioides cornutus*], young and old, male and female, curled up against the woodwork or domiciled in silken nests. I called our skipper's attention and his wonder at once ceased. He had innocently thought that clearing away the webs had disposed of the weavers. He had never imagined what a colony of unbidden passengers or 'stowaways' he was carrying.

In Europe, McCook's contemporary, Jean Henri Fabre (see Chapter 7), found that spiders *never, never* repair their webs. But McCook was sure that they could. He gave a diagram of how it is done and wrote:

> In the act of capturing an insect it becomes necessary for the spider to piece together the parts of the web which are separated either by the breakage of the insect's struggle or by the intentional cutting of the spider herself. This mending is done with great deftness and skill. The broken parts are held together by one or more of the feet, usually the hind feet. The claws on one side of the body grasp one portion of the armature, while those on the other grasp the opposite broken part. At the same time a thread thrown out from the spinnerets, is attached to margins of the fracture, and the rent is pieced together in a manner almost impossible to describe, and indeed to observe at all, so rapidly is it accomplished.

McCook dealt with every conceivable aspect of web-building behaviour. The triangle-web spider (*Hyptiotes*) occupied a whole chapter and no fewer than four chapters were devoted to the subject of egg cocoon construction. McCook described for the first time the great dome web of the Basilica spider (*Mecynogea*). He went into microscopic detail on the subject of the sticky beads on silk lines of web weavers. He discussed at length the phenomenon of spiders which use the weight of stones to counter-balance their webs. And he waxed lyrical about the discovery of a veritable 'Spider Paradise'. He was conversant with all the literature and authors on spiders. He mentioned most frequently Hentz, the Peckhams, Simon, Pickard-Cambridge, Blackwall, Moggridge and Darwin. Sometimes, however, he was mistaken; for example, he doubted the existence of social spiders as described by Darwin in South America.

Some of McCook's colourful observations are quite theatrical, for example – *the bee which escaped*. He related:

I chanced to get a sight of Argiope cophinaria [=*Argiope aurantia*] just as she had captured a large honey bee and had begun to swathe it. I watched the struggles of the insect and found that the spider got the better of her antagonist very rapidly. Around and around the excited bee the swathing bands wound, until at last it was completely enclosed within a silken bag. I concluded that all was over with the luckless insect, an opinion which Cophinaria evidently shared, for she laid on her final lines and clambered away to the centre of her shield, apparently with the intention of drawing her victim towards her to take a hearty meal.

Scarcely had she settled herself however, ere the bee renewed its struggles. In a moment it succeeded in cutting a little opening at one end of the sac, out of which first issued jaws, then antennae, then its head, and then its body. It was free. Instead of flying away, as one would have thought a reasonable insect ought to do, the bee turned with angry gestures upon the little ball of white silk into which had collapsed the enswathments out of which it had just escaped. Upon this she fastened her claws, thrust her sting ferociously into it several times, and then, as though she had satisfied her sense of justice and vengeance, spread her wings and began to ascend.

There was an angry hum in her wings, and an ugly look in the still outthrust sting, which led me to step back a pace or two lest I might come in for a share of her wrath. She followed me for a little distance and then, changing her mind, mounted into the air, and in a moment or two was hovering over a fragrant honeysuckle blossom, apparently solacing herself for her recent insult by the sweets of nectar. What an escapade that was! And, if the bee only knew it, what a story of 'hairbreadth escapes' she might have told to her comrades of the hive when she returned home.

McCook's original wish was to write a natural history, in one volume, of all North American spiders. However, it became obvious that it was impossible to cover everything. He therefore decided to modify the original plan and to concentrate on the orb-web spinners. That this group came to occupy three, packed volumes is a tribute to McCook *and* to the spiders.

FREDERICK PICKARD-CAMBRIDGE

Frederick Pickard–Cambridge (1860–1905) is the only well-known spider specialist to have commited suicide with his own gun. He was born in Warmwell, Dorset, England, and educated at Sherborne School and Exeter College, Oxford. Frederick was the nephew of the Reverend Octavius Pickard-Cambridge. He began as curate at St Cuthbert's church but left to become a professional artist working for various biologists. As a young man he was overflowing with enthusiasm for natural history, cricket and shooting. He spent a lot of time at the British Museum. In 1894 to 1895 he travelled for several months on the Amazon, as a naturalist aboard the SS *Faraday*, a cable-laying ship belonging to Alexander Siemens.

The spiders discovered during the expedition of the *Faraday* were described not in a single book but in a number of papers. In the first paper (1896) Pickard-Cambridge wrote:

> The identification of members of this order is by no means the easy matter one would suppose ... In the forest, Epeirids, Therididae, and Salticids swarm, of every shape and hue ... We have nothing to compare with the curious Gastracanthids, the crimson-spined *Micrathena schreibersi*, or

the numerous species of the thorny-backed genus *Gasteracantha*. We have nothing to match the huge *Nephila* with her diminutive husband, or the lovely *Argiope argentata* stretched on the white silken cross in the centre of its orbicular snare. Except an *Atypus* or two, we have nothing to take the place of the 250 species and upwards of the *Mygalomorphae* which are found in Southern and Central America. So that, although many a familiar form will meet the eye of the English arachnologist on the Amazons, yet there are countless forms differing in size, in structure, and in colour from anything that he can find amongst the Spider-fauna of Northern Europe . . . One must confess, too, that at the present time arachnologists still know *next to nothing* of the Spiders of Brazil . . . for instance, we do not yet know the staple diet of so common and so well-known a Spider as the huge *Avicularia*. Though I watched, on several occasions the whole night through, the tunnels of twenty and upwards of the sand-burrowing '*Mygale*', so common in the neighbourhood of Santarem, yet not *once* could I detect a Spider in the act of seizing her prey or even venturing beyond the entrance of her burrow.

I accentuate these deficiencies in our information, because one so often hears of a traveller neglecting to collect material, or make observations of habits, on the grounds that the 'Authorities' at home nowadays know *everything* and that the trouble taken would be but labour lost.

Unfortunately, Pickard-Cambridge's enthusiasm for life left him during his thirties. He developed ideas about religion which were out of step with Church of England orthodoxy and thus had to resign his Holy Orders. Extreme political views separated him from family and friends and arguments over classification led to quarrels with colleagues. When his life ended tragically in 1905, spiderology lost one of its most brilliant devotees – almost certainly he would have followed Reginald Innes Pocock in the position of arachnologist at the British Museum.

The death of Frederick Pickard-Cambridge was reported in *The Times* of 1905 under the heading: MENTAL STRAIN:

> An inquest was held at Wimbledon, yesterday afternoon, on Frederick Pickard-Cambridge, B.A., F.Z.S., aged forty-four, a naturalist. Major Edward Cambridge, of the Bedfordshire Regiment, brother, described the deceased as a cheerful, robust man, and unmarried. He had published several works, and had only recently finished a new volume. Last Thursday evening, after passing the day uneasily, and taking an unusually frugal dinner, he retired to his bedroom, where he was subsequently found dead with a bullet wound in the top of the head, and a pipe in one hand and a revolver in the other. He had a substantial banking account, and no cause other than mental strain could be assigned for the act. A verdict of 'Suicide while temporarily insane' was returned.

WILLIAM S. BRISTOWE

William Syer Bristowe (1901–79) was a unique figure in the history of arachnology. He was born in Surrey, England, and educated at Wellington College and Cambridge. He took part in university expeditions to Brazil and the Arctic and later travelled widely in his spare time. His enthusiasm for hunting spiders on romantic islands such as Krakatoa, Bear Island and Deserte Grande near Madeira, and his lively style of writing on a vast breadth of spider aspects has undoubtedly inspired many followers. He wrote several books and over 100 papers – mostly published before 1950 – on subjects such as courtship and mating (now often quoted), classification, folklore and the giant trap-door spider of South-East Asia (*Liphistius*). He is quoted in this book on many subjects. In 1964 he was presented by the Duke of Edinburgh with the first of the Stamford Raffles Awards for distinguished amateur zoologists.

The giant trap-door spider – a living fossil which resembles spiders of the Carboniferous Period – was one of Bristowe's greatest interests. He wrote: 'Illustrations of *Liphistius* fired my imagination as a school boy and ten years later, in 1930, I happened to be sent to Malaya on business. This gave me the opportunity to search in Penang for *Liphistius desultor* which had escaped capture since 1875.'

The nest of *Liphistius* is almost impossibly difficult to see. It is a foot-deep burrow hidden by a camouflaged trap-door with six to eight silk threads radiating from it as 'fishing lines' to detect passing insects. Bristowe described the capture of prey from one nest found in a shaky bank of earth:

> The first sign of the spider's presence is a slight quiver of the door as it detects the direction of its prey and prepares to rush out, which it does very quickly. The prey is seized, the spider turns round, rushes back carrying the prey, lifts the door instantaneously with its legs and disappears again. During this sortie it trails a thread which, in time, causes the 'fishing lines' to be stouter. The trailed thread, hooks and numerous stiff spines on the spider's legs remove the risk of falling and give the spider a very firm grip, as I know from the difficulty I had in shaking one off my finger.

Bristowe searched for *Liphistius* in Malaysia, Thailand and Sumatra, where it was known to occur; and also, to explore its potential distribution, in the Philippines and Sri Lanka. In these places he had no luck; however, *Liphistius* was not, and still is not, known to occur on those islands. *Liphistius* currently numbers 15 species, including *Liphistius bristowei*, named after his death.

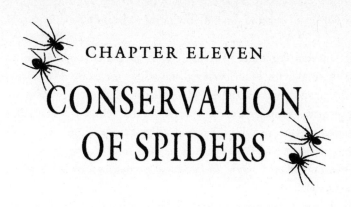

CHAPTER ELEVEN

CONSERVATION
OF SPIDERS

THE WORLD NEEDS SPIDERS

In China, every autumn, farmers build little huts out of straw – to house hibernating spiders beside the paddy-fields. The Chinese were the first to use spiders in the control of pests; by protecting them in little huts, the spiders survive the winter and are ready early in the spring to attack the hordes of insects which damage the crops. In Poland they too have cultivated spiders for many years. Now, other countries are also catching on, and in the search for an alternative to chemical insecticides, growers are increasingly turning to spiders as useful allies.

Spiders are more important to man in the balance of nature than most other groups of animals. This is perhaps especially true in the tropics where spiders are particularly abundant. They eat vast numbers of pests and are themselves the food of birds, etc. If the natural balance is upset, insect pests are capable of multiplying so quickly that they will completely consume a food crop. Many insects reproduce prolifically to offset the high death rates they face in nature. Because of natural predators, like spiders, rates of 99 per cent mortality in an insect generation are normal. Without predators, a pest population explosion can be expected. Unfortunately, the natural balance between insect pests and spiders is often disrupted by an indiscriminate use of chemical insecticides.

Humans have a choice: conserve spiders as allies in the battle against destructive insect pests – and tolerate occasional spiders in fruit and vegetables – or risk chemical residues on their food. Compared with other such natural allies, for example parasitic wasps, spiders tend to be generalist feeders – they feed on whatever is abundant, and it must be admitted that they sometimes attack each other and other beneficial species. After all, predators also have enemies of their own – other predators, parasites and pathogens. In fact most predators are cannibalistic, particularly spiders.

Progress has been made in understanding the role of spiders; in and around rice fields, at the International Rice Research Institute in the Philippines. In rice, spiders are useful because they search the plants for pests such as leafhoppers, planthoppers, moths and caterpillars. Spiders prefer moving prey but some will attack insect eggs. In the 'front line' are the wolf spiders (Lycosidae), each individual consuming about 5–15 small insects per day. Other day-active hunters are jumping spiders (Salticidae), which consume 4–8 green leafhoppers per day; and lynx spiders (Oxyopidae) which take 2–3 moths a day. There are also night hunters and web builders (Araneidae, Tetragnathidae and Linyphiidae) which, day or night, collect whatever comes. Research has found that it is not practical to mass-rear spiders for release in rice fields. Instead the idea is to use those which are naturally available – they simply need to be encouraged.

William Whitcomb, a spider enthusiast of Florida, is working with wolf spiders. He found that setting aside strips of weeds around fields of crops leaves the spiders a suitable home ground, from which they will patrol the fields. Wolf spiders are highly mobile and readily colonise new fields. They prey on pests before the latter can increase to damaging levels. In California, the wolf spider (*Pardosa ramulosa*) is an important predator of leafhopper insects. The leafhopper is a rice pest and it has been shown that if 20 spiders per square yard (1 sq m) are introduced to the fields, the pest is reduced in numbers by up to 90 per cent. In Britain, money spiders are helping to protect fields of winter wheat from hungry aphids. The Institute of Horticultural Research has discovered that the spiders weave horizontal webs among the stalks and, in effect, net the aphids when they fall. Also, the spiders are active earlier in the year than the other pest-controllers – ladybirds.

Agriculturalists are finding that spiders should be encouraged generally in crops, orchards, vineyards, plantations and forests. The way to do it is by cultivating suitable plants on the ground which will increase the numbers of spiders, or by simply leaving sufficient natural cover for them around the crops.

THE HEALTH OF THE PLANT

It is standard practice to describe and analyse environments in terms of their vegetation. Now, according to Dr Clausen of Denmark, it seems that spiders are one of the groups of animals that could be used as ecological indicators – though they are difficult for non-specialists to identify. Being mobile and relatively short-lived, spiders may adjust more rapidly to changes in the environment than plants and lichens. Furthermore, as spiders are predators, they have the potential for acquiring a biological concentration of toxic matter such as heavy metals. In Denmark, lead concentration in the spider *Nuctenea umbraticus* is as good a measure of the atmospheric lead level as it is in the lichen *Lecanora conizaeoides*. It has been noted that spider numbers drop in forests with high levels of atmospheric sulphur dioxide, though this may be a result of the reduction in plant richness, particularly lichens.

RED DATA LIST (ENDANGERED ANIMALS)

In the 1990 IUCN Red List, sixteen species of spiders around the world are quoted as 'threatened', including the Great Raft Spider (*Dolomedes plantarius*) of northern Europe, and the No-eyed Big-eyed Wolf Spider (*Adelocosa anops*) of the USA. But this small number of sixteen cannot possibly reflect the true number of species threatened with extinction, or already extinct. One could add a couple of noughts, or even three to that figure. Because of pollution and habitat destruction, the number and diversity of spiders is under serious threat – we need to protect them.

One species of spider is placed on the CITES schedule (Convention on International Trade in Endangered Species). It is the Mexican red-kneed Tarantula, *Brachypelma smithi* (family Theraphosidae). This is a beautiful species which has been over-collected for the pet trade. The species, endemic to Mexico, is placed in Appendix II, which requires that a permit is issued by Mexico for each spider exported to a CITES-observing country. Unfortunately, scientific data about its present-day status in the world – N. W. Mexico: Chiapas, Sonora, Guerrero, Colima, Nayarit, Mexico States – is 'insufficiently known'.

A unique breeding programme for the Mexican red knee is under way at London Zoo (Invertebrate Conservation Centre). Their links with other institutions, and their genetically diverse breeding stock, means that success is ensured. According to Dave Clark: 'In the wild mortality rates can be as high as 98 per cent; in captivity they may be as low as 2 per cent.' Furthermore, each mating results in more than 700 baby spiderlings.

THE DRINKS INDUSTRY

In France, cob-web spiders (*Tegenaria*) are cultivated and released into wine cellars to add that necessary, 'authentic' ambience. In Brussels, an old-fashioned beer brewery claims that spiders play an important role in controlling the number of fruit flies (*Drosophila*) which carry unwanted foreign micro-organisms, causing a different kind of fermentation and spoiling the beer. Rudi Jocque relates:

> Visitors to the attics, where the barrels with fermenting beers are kept, are often impressed by the huge number of spider webs covering walls, ceilings, barrels and everything . . . These webs obviously form a kind of screen preventing too high a number of insects from reaching the barrels and the beer, thus maintaining the balance in favour of the endemic yeasts. Killing a spider in the brewery is therefore regarded as an offence and everything is done to keep their populations high.

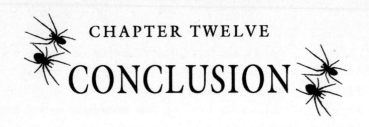

CHAPTER TWELVE

CONCLUSION

SPIDERS SHOULD BE VALUED

Spiders are a most colourful and talented breed. Evolution has fitted them for a vast range of habitats and lifestyles. They exist in all regions of the world and, via their 'ballooning', they have reached and colonised islands everywhere (probably spiders are absent only on the ice-cap of Antarctica). Many of the Earth's most inhospitable environments, from the hottest deserts to the frozen slopes near the summit of Mount Everest, have their own particular species of spiders. Deep in the earth, in the darkest caves, there are blind and often totally unique species. In 1989, new species of spiders were discovered in the Movile Cave of Romania. This cave has no natural opening to the outside and its food chain is based on the sulphurous waters which bubble up inside. At the other end of the spectrum, from the very rare species, many other kinds of spiders are found abundantly and close to man, in places such as plantations, sewage farms and buildings.

Without spiders in all their great variety, the world would be a poorer place. We would miss their beauty and their ingenuity. The more that people know about spiders and care about them the better. Of course, the conservation of their habitats is essential. In threatened habitats, the presence of rare species of spiders, which may capture the public's imagination, can add to the reasons why a habitat should be saved. At the same time, however, common spiders should not be neglected lest they will also disappear. We should encourage the ordinary kinds like typical wolf spiders and orb-weavers. They can be allies in the search for safe forms of pest control. Research is continually discovering remarkable things about spiders. For example, the way the jumping spider *Portia* is able to stalk its prey, sometimes losing sight of it, shows a considerable problem-solving ability for a creature which is less than one centimetre long.

SPIDERS ARE WORLDLY WISE

We can learn many things from spiders. Their patience and determination is legendary. Robert the Bruce was greatly inspired when he observed a 'wee beastie' trying repeatedly to get a line across a gap in the roof of a barn. And spiders have often lent inspiration to the language, with expressions such as 'a spider's touch' and 'the web of corruption'. Such metaphors seem to be used more and more as human life increasingly imitates the ways of the spider. The predatory, competitive way of life, the cunning tactics, the squatters and the thieves – all are familiar to both communities.

Spiders are skilled and versatile engineers. There are many parallels between human constructions and the building of webs, particularly orb-webs and scaffolding webs. Using their silk, with its unique properties, spiders are masters of the science of tensions, joints and supports. In webs, balance and stability is extremely important. In order to restore stability some orb-weaving spiders can patch over holes. With the benefit of hindsight, it appears that Fabre (1878) was mistaken and McCook (1889) was correct – orbweavers can indeed repair their webs. One species in fact, *Uloborus diversus*, has been shown by Bill Eberhard to be capable of making elaborate reconstructions of as much as half the web. The spider gathers together the tattered ends of the torn part to form a seam between the good half and the new half. In the rebuilt half, the spiral thread turns at the seam in a series of *turning points*.

Spiders are a rich natural resource. Their silks and venoms have many potential uses in biotechnology. Spider venom, which varies in composition from species to species, has a future in the production of environmentally safe insecticides. Also, it is expected that drugs derived from the venom of spiders, as well as snakes and other creatures, will be able to save the lives of future heart attack victims – through an immediate effect on the blood vessels, allowing the blood to flow more easily. The fact that spiders are themselves highly sensitive to drugs, and can contribute to an understanding of drug action, was discovered by a German zoologist in 1948. The story goes that Professor Hans Peters was bothered by the fact that his garden spiders always built their webs around 4 o'clock in the morning. He asked his colleague from Pharmacology, Dr Peter Witt, for a stimulant which, when fed to the spiders, could advance the hour of their work. Unfortunately, the resulting 'drugged webs' showed crazy distortions but there was no change in the hour of construction. The team tested a variety of drugs and found that web construction is highly sensitive to most of them, including amphetamines, LSD, caffeine and Valium. Certain drugs in low doses produced characteristic distortions of webs which could be specifically recognised.

FROM ARACHNOPHOBIA TO THE LOVE OF SPIDERS

Arachnophobia is common but for many people, spiders are fascinating; children, in particular, find them exciting. Some of the varied relationships between man and spiders, present and past, have been explored in this book. Also the lives of some of the great adventurers and spider experts, going right back to Aristotle, have been remembered.

Spiders have many roles in folklore, stories and different kinds of entertainment. In clothing, footwear, jewellery,

furniture and other objects, designs have been inspired by spiders or their webs. Designers such as Schiaparelli, Makepeace and Dubreuil have all used the web as a source of inspiration. The patterns of webs with their straight and spiral lines have also had a direct influence on makers of lace. In some countries spiders are popular as contestants in gladiatorial sports, in other countries they are a culinary treat. Countless movies have featured spiders and some of the most memorable have included: *Sherlock Holmes and the Spider Woman* (1946), *Horrors of Spider Island* (1962), *Charlotte's Web* (1973), *Tarantulas: the Deadly Cargo* (1977), *Kiss of the Spider Woman* (1989) and, not for the nervous, *Arachnophobia* (1990).

It is the author's hope that one day there will be a spider's version of the butterfly hot-house. Delightful as it is to be able to walk among butterflies, it would be a similar pleasure to have spiders at every turn. Spectacular but harmless species, necessarily of the kind that stay put in webs, could happily live together in a jungle-like environment, and some might even hang from the ceiling. It would be great fun *and* educational – the reason why spiders cause so much anxiety and arachnophobia is that they are not understood. Such a tropical spider house would enable us to debunk all those hackneyed horror stories of cross-breeding different species to produce killer hybrids, which then multiply out of control with dreadful consequences . . . All nonsense!

REFERENCES

CHAPTER ONE

Beerman, H. and Nutting, W. B. 1984. 'Arachnid-related phobias: symbiophobia, prevention and treatment': 103–112, in Nutting, W. B. (Ed.) *Mammalian Diseases and Arachnids* vol. 2, *Medico-veterinary, laboratory, and wildlife diseases and control*, CRC Press Inc., Boca Raton, Florida.

Davy, G. [City University of London] 1992. 'The "unclean" theory of arachnophobia' (*Daily Telegraph* report).

Freud, S. 1971. *The Complete Introductory Lectures on Psychoanalysis*, George Allen & Unwin, London.

Hardy, T. N. 1988. 'Entomophobia: the case for Miss Muffet', *Bull. Entomol. Soc. Am.* 34: 64–69.

Kellert, S. & Westervelt, M. 1981. *Children's Attitudes, Knowledge and Behaviours Towards Animals*, US Department of the Interior (Fish & Wildlife Service).

Levi, P. 1989. 'The Fear of Spiders', in *Other People's Trades*, 141–5, Abacus, London.

Mother Goose, 1916. *The Real Mother Goose*, Rand McNally, Chicago.

Paterson, D. and Palmer, M. (Eds.) 1989. *The Status of Animals – Ethics, Education and Welfare*, C.A.B. International, Wallingford.

Savory, T. H. 1961. *Spiders, Men and Scorpions*, London University Press.

CHAPTER TWO

Anderson, J. C. 1928. *Myths and Legends of the Polynesians*, Harrap, London.

Beavis, I. C. 1988. *Insects and Other Invertebrates in Classical Antiquity*, Exeter University Publications.

Caillois, R. 1972. *Le Mythe et l'homme*, Gallimard, Paris.

Cloudsley-Thompson, J. L. 1988. 'The study of spider mythology and folklore', *Country-side, Journal of the British Naturalists' Association*, 26: 4–6.

Cunninghame Graham, R. B. *Conquest of New Granada.*

De Rosny, E. 1981. *Les Yeux de ma chevre*, Editions Plon, Collection Terre Humaine, Paris.

France, P. and Hosking, E. and D. 1986. *An Encyclopaedia of Bible Animals*, Steimatz Ltd, Tel Aviv.

Hudson, W. H. 1892. *The Naturalist in La Plata*, Chapman and Hall, London.

Jung, C. G. 1964. *L'Homme et ses symboles*, Laffont, Paris.

Levi, P. 1989. 'The Fear of Spiders', in *Other People's Trades*, 141–5, Abacus, London.

Mackenzie, D. A. 1931. *Myths from Melanesia and Indonesia*, Gresham Publishing, London.

Savory, T. H. 1961. *Spiders, Men and Scorpions*, London University Press.

Sherlock, P. M. 1956. *Anansi the Spider Man*, Macmillan, London.

Siganos, A. 1985. *Les Mythologies de l'insecte*, Librairie des Meridiens, Paris.

Stone, M. 1979. *Ancient Mirrors of Womanhood*, New Sibylline Books, New York.

Thomas, D. L. & L. B. 1920. *Kentucky Superstitions*, Princeton University Press, New Jersey.

Tongiorgi, P. 1986. 'The iconography of the spider in manuscripts and printed books between the 15th and 17th centuries', *Actas X Congr. Int. Arachnol.* Jaca/España, 1: 65.

Topsell, E. 1607, 1658. *Four-footed Beasts and Animals.*

White, E. B. 1952. *Charlotte's Web*, Hamish Hamilton Children's Books, London.

CHAPTER THREE

Aristotle, *Historia Animalium* [see Chapter 9, Wentworth Thompson].

Bristowe, W. S. 1930. 'The distribution and dispersal of spiders'. *Proc. Zool. Soc. Lond*, 4: 633–657.

Darwin, C. 1845. *The Voyage of the Beagle* ('A naturalist's voyage around the world'), J. M. Dent & Co., London, publ. 1906.

Eberhard, W. G. 1987. 'How spiders initiate airborne lines', *J. Arachnol*, 15: 1–9.

Emerton, J. H. 1919. 'The flights of spiders in the autumn of 1918', *Ent. News*, 30: 165–168.

Gertsch, W. J. 1979. *American Spiders*, Van Nostrand Reinhold Co., New York.

Holzapfel, E. P. and Perkins, B. D. 1969. 'Trapping of air-borne insects on ships in the Pacific', *Pacific Insects*, 11 (2): 455–476.

McCook, H. C. 1889–94. *American Spiders and their Spinningwork*, published by the author, Philadelphia.

Parker, J. and Harley, B. (Eds.) 1992. *Martin Lister's English Spiders*, Harley Books, Colchester.

Phillpotts, J. S. 1984. 'Flying spiders'. *Entomologist's Record*, 96: 214–215.

White, G. 1788. *The Natural History and Antiquities of Selborne*, B. White and Son, London.

CHAPTER FOUR

Baerg, W. J. 1923. 'The effect of the bite of *Latrodectus mactans*' Fabr., *J. Parasitol.*, 9: 161–169.

Baerg, W. J. 1958. *The Tarantula*, University of Kansas Press.

Baerg, W. J. 1959. *The Black Widow and Five other Venomous Spiders in the United States*, University of Arkansas, *Bull.* 608.

Charpentier, P. 1992. *Vogelspinnen in hun natuurlijke omgeving: 1 Africa*, Exothermae Publications, Belgium.

Duffey, E. and Green, M. B. 1975. A linyphiid spider biting workers on a sewage-treatment plant. *Bull. Brit. Arach. Soc.* 3(5): 130–1

Lucas, S. 1988. 'Spiders in Brazil', *Toxicon*, 26: 759–772.

Peters, W. 1992. *A Colour Atlas of Arthropods in Clinical Medicine*, Wolfe Publ. Ltd, London.

Quicke, D. 1988. 'Spiders bite their way to safer insecticides', *New Scientist*, 1640: 38–41.

Raven, R. J. 1992. 'White-tailed spiders and the mystery necrotic lesions', Queensland Museum information sheet.

Riley, C. V. and Howard, L. O. 1889. 'A contribution to the literature of fatal spider bites', *Insect Life*, 1: 204–211.

Russell, F. E. 1988. 'Venomous animals' injuries', in Schachner and Handsen, (Eds.), *Pediatric Dermatology*, Churchill Livingstone.

Savory, T. H. 1961. *Spiders, Men and Scorpions*, University of London Press.

Scott, G. 1980. *The Funnelweb*, Darling Downs Institute Press, Toowoomba.

Thorp, R. W. and Woodson, W. D. 1945. *Black Widow, America's most poisonous spider*, University of North Carolina Press.

CHAPTER FIVE

Anima, Nid. 1982. 'And now, spider fighting', *Manila Magazine.*
Bristowe, W. S. 1932. 'Insects and other invertebrates for human consumption in Siam', *Trans. Ent. Soc. London*, 80: 387–404.
LaBillardière, H. de, 1800. *An account of a Voyage in Search of La Perouse undertaken by order of the Constituent Assembly of France and Performed in the Years 1791, 1792 and 1793*, London.
Quinn, P. J. 1959. *Food and feeding habits of the Pedi*, Witwatersrand University Press, Johannesburg.
West, R. 1992. 'Not to everyone's taste', *Forum American Tarant. Soc*, 1 (2). (J. Brit. Tarant. Soc. 8 (2): 26–27.)

CHAPTER SIX

Abraham N. 1923. 'Observations on Fish- and Frog-eating Spiders of Natal', *Ann. Natal Mus.*, 5: 88–94.
Berg, C. 1883. 'Eine fischende Spinne', *Kosmos* 13: 375.
Blest, A. D. and Land, M. F. 1977. 'The physiological optics of *Dinopis subrufus* L.Koch: a fish-lens in a spider', *Proc. R. Soc. Lond.*, B. 196: 197–222.
Buskirk, R. E. 1981. 'Sociality in the Arachnida', 281–359, in Hermann, H. R. (Ed.) *Social Insects*, vol 2.
Chisholm, J. R. see McKeown, K. C. 1952 below.
Clagget, G. 1914. 'A spider swathing mice'. *Entomological News*, 25: 230.
Darchen, R. and Delage-Darchen, B. 1986. 'Societies of spiders compared to the societies of insects', *J. Arachnol.* 14: 227–238.
Dover, C. 1932. 'A social spider as a pest of mango trees'. *Indian Forester*, 58: 615–16.
Eberhard, W. G. 1977. 'Aggressive chemical mimicry by a bolas spider', *Science*, 198: 1173–1175.
Fink, L. S. 1984. 'Venom spitting by the green lynx spider, *Peucetia viridans* (Araneae, Oxyopidae)', *J. Arachnol.*, 12: 372–73.
Gertsch, W. J. 1954. 'Houdini of the spider world', in Neider, C. (Ed.), *The Fabulous Insects*, Harper & Brothers, New York.
Henschel, J. R. 1990. 'Spiders wheel to escape predators', *S. Afr. J. Sci.*, 86:
Hillyard, P. D. 1989. 'In a fish tank in a pet shop in Grimsby: *Desis martensi* L.Koch imported among coral', *Newsl. Br. Arachnol. Soc.*, 55: 1–2.

Jackson, R. R. and Blest, A. D. 1982. 'The distances at which a primitive jumping spider, *Portia fimbriata*, makes visual discriminations', *J. Exp. Biol.*, 97: 441–445.

Jackson, R. R. and Hallas, S. E. A. 1986. 'Comparative biology of *Portia africana*, *P. albimana*, *P. fimbriata*, *P. labiata*, and *P. shultzi*, araneophagic, web-building jumping spiders (Araneae: Salticidae): utilisation of webs, predatory versatility, and intraspecific interactions', *N. Z. J. Zool.*, 13: 423–489.

Jambunathan, N. S. 1905. 'The habits and life history of a social spider (*Stegodyphus sarasinorum* Karsch)', *Smithson. Misc. Coll.*, 47: 365–372.

Land, M. F. 1985. 'The morphology and optics of spider eyes', in Barth F. G. (Ed.) *Neurobiology of Arachnids*, 53–78. Springer Verlag, Berlin.

McKeown, K. C. 1952. *Spider Wonders of Australia*, Angus & Robertson, Sydney.

Main, B. Y. 1976. *Spiders*, The Australian Naturalist Library, Collins, Sydney.

Moggridge, J. T. 1873. *Harvesting ants and Trap-door spiders. Notes and observations on their habits and dwellings*, L. Reeve & Co., London.

Peckham, G. W. and E. 1887. 'Some observations on the mental powers of spiders', *Journ. Morph.*, 1 (2): 383–419.

Pocock, R. I. 1900. 'The Great Indian Spiders', *J. Bombay Nat. Hist.* 13: 121.

Raven, R. 1990. 'Spider predators of reptiles and amphibia', *Mem. Queensland Mus.*, p. 448.

Richman, D. B. and Jackson, R. R. 1992. 'A review of the ethology of jumping spiders (Araneae, Salticidae)', *Bull. Br. arachnol. Soc.*, 9 (2): 33–37.

Riper, van W. 1946. 'How strong is the Trapdoor spider?' *Natural History*.

Rovner, J. S. 1986. 'Spider hairiness: air stores and low activity enhance flooding survival in inland terrestrial species', *Actas X Congr. Int. Arachnol.*, Jaca/Espana, 1: 123–129.

Steyn, J. J. 1959. 'Use of social spiders against gastro-intestinal infections spread by house flies', *South African Medical Journal*, 33: 730–731.

Vellard, J. 1936. *Le Venin des araignées*, Monographies de l'Institut Pasteur, Masson et Cie, Paris.

Vollrath, F. 1987. 'Kleptobiosis in spiders', in Nentwig, W. (Ed.) *Ecophysiology of spiders*, 274–286, Springer Verlag, Berlin/Heidelberg.

Wanless, F. R. 1975. 'Spiders of the family Salticidae from the upper slopes of Everest and Makalu'. *Bull. Br. Arachnol. Soc.*, 3: 132–36.

CHAPTER SEVEN

Albertis, L. M. d' 1880. *New Guinea: What I did and what I saw*, vols. 1 & 2, Sampson Low, Marston, Searle & Rivington, London.

Beard, J. 1992. 'Warding off bullets by a spider's thread', *New Scientist*, 14 Nov. 1992.

Camboué, P. 1892. 'La soie d'Araignée', *Rev. Sci. nat. appl.*, 39: 299–306.

Cunningham, D. D. 1907. *Plagues and Pleasures of Life in Bengal*, London.

Decae, A. E. 1984. 'A theory on the origin of spiders and the primitive function of silk', *J. Arachnol.*, 12: 21–28.

Eberhard, W. G. 1981. 'Construction behaviour and the distribution of tensions in orb webs', *Bull. Br. Arachnol. Soc.*, 5: 189–204.

Fabre, J. H. (translated by A. Teixeira de Mattos) 1939. *The Life of the Spider*, Hodder and Stoughton, London.

Foelix, R. F. 1982. *Biology of Spiders*, Harvard University Press, Cambridge, Mass.

Gaggin, J. 1900. *Among the Man-eaters*, London.

Gosline, J. M. *et al.* 1984. 'Spider silk as rubber', *Nature*, 309: 551–552.

Gudger, E. W. 1918. 'The most remarkable fishing net known – the spider's web net', *Zool. Soc. Bull.*, 21: 1588–90.

Guppy, H. B. 1887. *The Solomon Islands and their Natives*.

Hillyard, P. D. 1983. 'Rediscovery of *Episinus maculipes* (Araneae: Theridiidae)', *Bull. Br. Arachnol. Soc.*, 6 (2): 88–92.

Hingston, R. W. G. 1920. *A Naturalist in the Himalaya*, Witherby, London.

Lewis, R. *et al.* 1992. 'The structure of spider silk', *Accounts of Chemical Research*, 25: 392–398.

Meek, A. S. 1913. *A Naturalist in Cannibal Land*, T. Fisher Unwin, London.

Moreau, R. E. 1936. 'Bird-Insect Nesting Associations', *Ibis*, 6 (3): 460–471.

Palmer, J. 1991. 'Wondrous spiders', *Threads Magazine*, 34: 24.

Peters, P. J. 1970. 'Orb-web construction: Interaction of spider (*Araneus diadematus* Cl.) and thread configuration', *Anim. Behav.*, 18: 478–84.

Pratt, E. A. 1906. *Two Years among New Guinea Cannibals.*

Priestly, H. E. 1979. *Truly Bizarre*, London.

Roberts, N. L. 1940. 'Bird/spider relationships', *Emu*, 39: 293–95.

Selden, P. A. 1983. 'The Biggest Spider', *Newsl. Br. Arach. Soc.* 36: 4–5.

Shear, W. A. (Ed.) (1986). *Spiders. Webs, Behavior, and Evolution*, Stanford University Press, California.

Shear, W. A., Palmer, J. M., Coddington, J. A. and Bonamo, P. M. (1989). 'A Devonian spinneret: early evidence of spiders and silk use', *Science*, 246: 479–481.

Sloane, H. 1725. *A Voyage to the Islands Madera, Barbados, Nieves, S. Christophers and Jamaica, with the Natural History of the Herbs and Trees, Four-footed beasts, Fishes, Birds, Insects, Reptiles etc. of the last those Islands*, London.

Stong, C. L. 1963. 'How to collect and preserve the delicate webs of spiders', *Scientific American*, Feb. 1963: 159–166.

Stowe, M. K. 1986. 'Prey specialization in the Araneidae', in Shear (1986), see above.

Witt, P. N., Scarboro, M. B. and Daniels, R. (1977). 'Spider web-building in outer space: evaluation of records from the Skylab spider experiment', *J. Arachnol.* 4: 115–124.

Witt, P. N. (1989). 'NASA, spiders and I', *Newsl. Am. Arach. Soc.*, 39: 2–3.

CHAPTER EIGHT

Azara, F. de 1809. *Voyages dans l'Amerique Meridionale*, vols 1–4, Dentu, Imprimeur-Librarie, Paris.

Bates, H. W. 1863. *The Naturalist on the River Amazons*, John Murray, London.

Bristowe, W. S. 1924. 'Notes on the habits of insects and spiders in Brazil', *Trans. Ent. Soc. Lond.*, 3,4: 475–505.

Darwin, C. 1845. *The Voyage of the Beagle* ('A naturalist's voyage around the world'), J. M. Dent & Co., London, publ. 1906.

Hingston, R. W. G. 1932. *A Naturalist in the Guiana Forest*, Edward Arnold & Co., London.

Masterman, G. F. 1888. *Seven Eventful Years in Paraguay.*

Oliveira, P. S. and Sazima, I. 1985 'Ant-hunting behaviour in spiders with emphasis on *Strophius nigricans* (Thomisidae), *Bull. Br. Arachnol. Soc.* 6: 309–312.

Oviedo, F. de 1855. *Historia General y Natural de las Indias.*

CHAPTER NINE

Beavis, I. C. 1988. *Insects and other invertebrates in Classical Antiquity*, Exeter University Press.
Bristowe, W. S. 1955. in Locket and Millidge (Eds.), *British Spiders*, Ray Society, London.
Coddington, J. A. and Levi, H. W. 1991. 'Systematics and Evolution of Spiders (Araneae)', *Annu. Rev. Ecol. Syst.*, 22: 565–92.
Jones-Walters, L. 1983. 'Mediaeval arachnology: The first English-speaking text?', *Newsl. Br. Arachnol. Soc.*, 37: 1–3.
Lister, Martin. *Tractatus de Araneis* (1678), translation: *Martin Lister's English Spiders*, Parker, J. et al. (1992).
McCook, H. 1889–94. *American Spiders and their Spinningwork*, published by the author, Philadelphia.
Macgillivray, W. 1834. *Lives of eminent zoologists*, Oliver & Boyd, Edinburgh.
Matthews, J. R. 1968. 'The life and works of France's greatest arachnologist', *Bull. Br. Spider Study Group*, 38: 1–6.
Pickard-Cambridge, A. W. 1918. *Memoir of the Reverend Octavius Pickard-Cambridge*, printed for private circulation, Oxford.
Savory, T. H. 1961. *Spiders, Men, and Scorpions*, University of London Press.
Swann, P. H. 1973. 'Thomas Mouffet's Theatrum Insectorum', 1634, *Bull. Brit. Arach. Soc.*, 2 (8): 169–173.
Victory, K. S. and Cokendolpher, J. C. 1989. 'On Carl Clerck's spider collection', *Newsl. Amer. Arachnol. Soc.*, 39.
Wentworth Thompson, D'Arcy, 1910. *The Works of Aristotle Translated into English*, vol. IV *Historia Animalium*, Clarendon Press, Oxford.

CHAPTER TEN

Bristowe, W. S. 1975. 'A family of living fossil spiders', *Endeavour*, 34: 115–117.
Hanley, Wayne. 1977. *Natural History in America*, Quadrangle/New York Times Book Co., (on N. Hentz).
McCook, H. 1889–94. *American Spiders and their Spinningwork*, published by the author, Philadelphia.

'Obituary-Henry Christopher McCook', *Entomological News* (1911), 22: 433–438.

Pickard-Cambridge, F. O. 1896. 'On the *Theraphosidae* of the Lower Amazons: being an account of the new Genera and Species of this Group of Spiders discovered during the Expedition of the Steamship "Faraday"', *Proceedings of the Zoological Society of London*.

CHAPTER ELEVEN

Allred, D. M. 1975. 'Arachnids as ecological indicators', *Gt. Basin Nat.*, 35: 405–6.

Clarke, D. 1991. 'Captive breeding programme for the Red-kneed bird-eating spider', *Int. Zoo. Yb.*, 30: 68–75.

Clausen, I. H. S. 1986. 'The use of spiders as ecological indicators', *Bull. Br. Arachnol. Soc.*, 7: 83–86.

IUCN (1990): *1990 IUCN Red List of Threatened Animals*, Gland, Cambridge: International Union for the Conservation of Nature.

Jocque, R. 1982. 'Spiders protecting endemic beer', *Newsl. Br. Arachnol. Soc.*, 33: 4.

Murphy, F. 1980. *Keeping Spiders, Insects and other Land Invertebrates in Captivity*, Bartholemew, Edinburgh.

Shepard, B. M., Barrion, A. T. and Litsinger, J. A. 1987. *Helpful Insects, Spiders, and Pathogens*, International Rice Research Institute, Manila.

Wells, S. M. *et al.* 1983. *The IUCN Invertebrate Red Data Book*, Gland, Cambridge: International Union for the Conservation of Nature.

CHAPTER TWELVE

Eberhard, W. G. 1972. 'The web of *Uloborus diversus* (Araneae, Uloboridae)', *J. Zool.*, (London) 166: 417.

Mertins, J. W. 1986. 'Arthropods on the Screen', *Bull. Entomol. Soc. Am.*, 32: 85–90.

Peters, H. M. and Witt, P. N. 1949. 'Die Wirkung von Substanzen auf den Netzbau der Spinnen', *Experientia*, (Basel) 5: 161.

Witt, P. N., Reed, C. F. and Peakall, D. B. 1968. *A Spider's Web – Problems in Regulatory Behaviour*, Springer Verlag, Berlin.

INDEX

Abbot, John, 160
Abrahams, Rev., 98
Académie des Sciences, Paris,
    152
aeronautic spiders, 41–8
    ballooning, 41–3, 44–5, 47–8
    becoming airborne, 44–5
    continued research, 47–8
    gossamer, phenomenon of, 45–7
    observations in historical times,
        43
Agelena, European, 114
Agelenidae family (cobweb weavers),
    76
Albertis, L. M. d', 100
Albin, Eleazar: *A Natural History of*
        Spiders and other curious
        Insects, 38, 39–40, 151
Aldrovandus, Ulysses, 35, 37, 146
    De Animalibus Insectis, 35, 37,
        146
Anansi the spider, story of, 30–1
anatomy of the spider, 77
Ancient Egyptians, 22–3
Andrewes, Laurence: *The Noble Lyfe*,
    144–5
Antofagasta, Chile, 49
Arachne, story of (Ovid), 16–17
arachnophobia (fear of spiders),
    3–14
    analyses and theories, 8–12
    assessing attitudes towards
        spiders, 7–8
    case histories, 6–7
    different kinds, 5
    therapeutic treatment, 12–14
Araneidae family, 112, 116, 172
    Araneus angulatus, 109, 110
    A. diadematus (garden spider),
        23, 105, 107, 119–20, 121,
        122, 146, 150, 152
    bolas spiders, 76, 92–3
    Celaenia, 92
    Mastophora, 92, 93, 117
    orb-web spiders, 76, 104–8
araneism syndrome, 62–4
Araniella, European, 116
Archemorus, Australian, 118
Argiope (wasp spider), x–xi, 69, 113,
    116

A. argentata, 168
A. aurantia, 165
A. bruennichi, 110
A. lobata, 110
Argyrodes, 118, 127
Argyroneta aquatica, 97
Aristotle, 29, 43, 142, 143, 178
    Génération des ánimaux, 139
    Historia Animalium, 138, 143
    scientific study of spiders,
        138–41
art, spiders in, 34–5
Ashmole, Elias, 38
Atrax robustus (Australian funnelweb
    spider), 61, 67
Atypus (purse-web spider), 113, 168
Aurengzebe, Emperor of Hindustan,
    121
Azara, Don Felix de, 95, 128, 129
    Voyages dans l'Amérique
        Meridionale, 126

Baerg, Dr, 60–1, 65, 66
Baglivi, Georges, 56, 58
Bannockburn, battle of, 25
Bates, Henry Walter, 130–3
    The Naturalist on the River
        Amazon, 132
Beauvois, Palisot de, 132
Beavis, Ian, 141
Berg, Carlos, 98
Berland, Lucien, 157
Bible, spiders in the, 23–4
Blackwell, John, 155, 165
    A History of the Spiders of Great
        Britain and Ireland, 149, 154
    classification of spiders, 153–4
Blest, Dr A. D., 93
Bloxworth, Dorset, 155
Bologna University Library, 35
Bon, Xavier Saint-Hilaire, 121
Brazil, Dr Vital, 81
Bristowe, Dr William Syer, 3fn, 29,
        47, 70, 71, 134–5, 169–70
British Library, 35
Browning, Dr, 60
Burgmann family, Innsbruck, 121–2
Buskirk, Ruth, 95
Byron, Lord: *The Prisoner of Chillon*,
    26

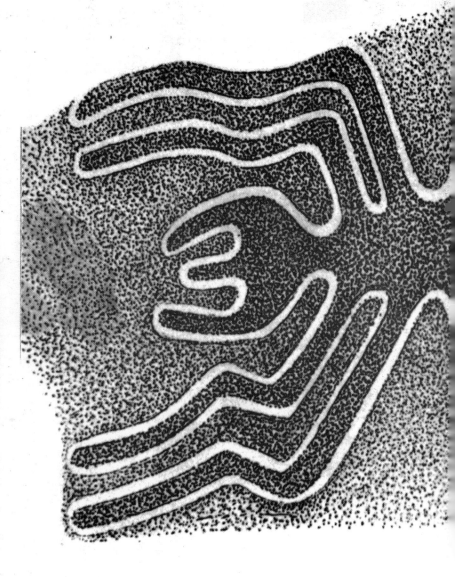